ID0990088

THE GREAT BOSTON FIRE

THE GREAT BOSTON FIRE

The Inferno That Nearly Incinerated the City

STEPHANIE SCHOROW

Globe
Pequot

Guilford, Connecticut

Globe Pequot

An imprint of Globe Pequot, the trade division of
The Rowman & Littlefield Publishing Group, Inc.
4501 Forbes Blvd., Ste. 200
Lanham, MD 20706
www.rowman.com

Distributed by NATIONAL BOOK NETWORK

British Library Cataloguing in Publication Information available
Library of Congress Cataloging-in-Publication Data
Names: Schorow, Stephanie, author.
Title: The Great Boston Fire : the inferno that nearly incinerated the city
   / Stephanie Schorow.
Description: Guilford, Connecticut : Globe Pequot, [2022] | Includes
   bibliographical references and index. | Summary: "The 1872 Great Boston
   Fire was barely contained after two days of spreading rapidly across the
   city, becoming one of the most expensive fire disasters in America"—
   Provided by publisher.
Identifiers: LCCN 2021044051 (print) | LCCN 2021044052 (ebook) | ISBN
   9781493054985 (hardback) | ISBN 9781493054992 (epub)
Subjects: LCSH: Great Fire, Boston, Mass., 1872. |
   Fires—Massachusetts—Boston.
Classification: LCC F73.5 .S36 2022 (print) | LCC F73.5 (ebook) | DDC
   974.4/61—dc23
LC record available at https://lccn.loc.gov/2021044051
LC ebook record available at https://lccn.loc.gov/2021044052

CONTENTS

"Don't Try to Magnify the Wants of Your Department"

Barely three weeks after the Great Fire had cooled, John Stanhope Damrell, head of the Boston Fire Department, was summoned to explain exactly why the city had nearly burned down on his watch.

He was not the first witness to be called by a five-man commission appointed by Boston Mayor William Gaston to investigate the Great Fire's cause and its management. Nor would he be the last. Just the most important. This being Boston, the commission would not rest until every nuance, every detail, could be wrangled out of witnesses to find out why the Athens of America—the birthplace of the American Revolution—had come so close to destruction.

Damrell hoped the five men who would hear his testimony were honorable men, reasonable men who would listen to him now, as other perhaps less reasonable men had not. He may have wished that rather than donning his formal frock jacket and tie, he could wear his battered and sooty helmet and his stained coat and boots to the hearing. It would be evidence of the lingering effect on him and every fireman who had fought the conflagration. He hoped his voice would not break; his throat was still recovering from the smoke and searing heat.

As he walked to the meeting with his satchel of papers, he found himself neither fearful nor hopeful. To be perfectly frank, he was still a bit numb from the sights and sounds of November 9, 10, and 11: the inhuman howl of the flames, the crack of exploding granite, the crash of falling brick, and the reassuring chugging from the steam fire engines, water hissing as it sprayed the fiery monster that seemed to have emerged from hell itself. He thought of his men, tiny dark figures against an orange backdrop, "playing" the fire, sending arches of water into the maws of totally engulfed structures. Again, and again, those streams failed to reach the tops of the buildings, and he had to watch as the flames jumped from roof to roof and block to block. In some ghastly moments, falling granite and brick landed on hoses, cutting off the streams. Worse yet, the water sometimes petered out altogether, leaving nothing between his men and the flames. The sight of those faltering streams would haunt him the rest of his life. He had long dreaded that exact occurrence and it was terrible to see his nightmare come true. He grieved for the firefighters and volunteers lost, all good men, from Boston, Cambridge, Malden, Charlestown, West Roxbury, and Worcester, and for the others nursing burns and scorched lungs.

As he was sworn in and readied himself for the commissioner's first question, he took comfort in knowing the ruins of the fire were no longer smoldering and the streets were being cleared of rubble. Merchants had even set up makeshift stores on the wrecks of their former businesses. Thank God for the insurance companies which, however reluctantly, were obligated to cover their subscribers' losses, even to the point of becoming insolvent. God bless New England pluck! He always admired the region's can-do attitude, the same attitude that helped catapult him from orphan to skilled carpenter to volunteer firefighter to assistant fire chief and, finally, to Chief Engineer of the Boston Fire Department.

Damrell regarded the faces of the commission members before him, men prominent in the city who had agreed to perform this duty. He knew most of them. They might be willing to listen to his explanations. Or perhaps they were simply looking for someone to blame.

Commissioner Thomas Russell asked the first question: How long had he been chief of the department?

"It will be seven years the first of April next—six years and nine months."

The questions flowed quickly after that: How did Damrell first hear about the fire? What was the condition of the fire when he arrived at the corner of Kingston and Summer Streets in downtown Boston?

Damrell took a deep breath. "Well, Sir, I have no language that I could [use to] describe it, really; suffice it to say, that the building was on fire from the basement to the top, presenting, as it were, one vast furnace. The heat was so intense on my arriving there, that it was impossible to get within fifty or seventy-five feet of the building. The material of the building being granite, its explosive properties were shown very conclusively by the shower of granite that was flying in every direction, from pieces weighing one pound to ten and twenty."

"I say this, and wish to be distinctly understood, that in my experience in the Boston Fire Department, covering twenty-five years, I never saw such a sight as was presented that night ... and I don't think there is a man in the fire department who ever did."

After more preliminary questions, Russell came to the issue that was really at hand: "State what, in your judgment, was the cause of the fire becoming uncontrollable."

So it begins, Damrell thought.

"It was uncontrollable from the fact that there was no alarm given until the building in which the fire originated was literally consumed, a matter which I think needs the most thorough and rigid examination," he said, keeping his language neutral and his tone even.

"The other causes?"

"The other causes that made it unmanageable were the scarcity of water and the extreme height of the buildings."

"What was the reason [for] the scarcity of water?"

"The inadequate size of the pipes to give the supply."

The commissioners pressed on. "Have you thought of any way of supplying that [water] except by increasing the size of the mains?"

Damrell gave a lengthy answer, explaining he had thought of many ways—installing larger water mains, using different kinds of hydrants and stationing more fire engine houses in the downtown commercial district, which although "comprising nearly all the wealth of Boston, has been largely destitute of steam fire engines." He spoke of building heights, how larger four- and five-story commercial buildings had taken over what was once a residential area.

"I have for quite a number of years regarded the buildings that have been constructed in Boston, especially the large warehouses, as being the instrument that would eventually destroy Boston," he said.

He brought with him his annual reports from the previous five years. He repeated what was in those reports: The districts were now inadequate to protect the newer intensive commercial development; the main of four and six inches should be at least eight inches in diameter. But, a commissioner asked, weren't there other districts just as thickly inhabited where water supply was the same? Yes, Damrell said, but not where the buildings had been built so high.

"I sent a written communication to the President of the Water Board upon this subject. He did not answer my communication in writing, but sent one of his clerks to me, saying, when they were in want of any suggestions from the Chief Engineer of the Fire Department, he would let me know."

He could not keep the pique out of his voice with that last remark.

The commissioners appeared unmoved. Perhaps, Damrell thought, they believed he was merely dissembling, trying to pass off blame. He returned to the issue of fire engines. There were simply not enough stationed downtown to protect the rapidly growing area. "No amount of influence that I could bring to bear has remedied the evil," he said.

"When did you bring that to the attention of the city?" Russell asked.

Damrell replied wearily, no longer concealing his frustration, "I have been constantly doing it for the last four or five years."

"Have you stated to the City Council what you have stated here?"

"I have said much about this matter. I have been met with the reply, 'Don't try to magnify the wants of your department or of your office so much.'"

The commissioners paused to consider what Damrell had said. Then Russell spoke—whether to challenge Damrell or to allow him to underscore his points cannot be determined from the transcript of the commission hearing.

"The idea of the City Government has been that they employed you to do a piece of work, not to tell them what should be done."

Was Damrell able to keep anger from his voice, the anger of a man who had devoted twenty-five years to the science and the art of firefighting? Did he speak with fierce indignation, thinking of how he had visited the smoking ruins of the Great Chicago Fire just a year earlier, and returned with the determination that what happened in Chicago should not happen in Boston? Or did he keep his composure, putting aside the thoughts of how his recommendations had fallen on so many deaf ears?

The transcript only shows his measured response.

"They did not consider my judgment worth entertaining."

Built on Ash

The Downtown Crossing area of Boston has always seemed like the heart of the city to me. I disagree with friends who prefer strolling the North End or the Public Garden or any of a number of other favorite hangouts. For me, the corners of Washington and Summer Streets beat with the city's pulse; retail, entertainment, tourism, and finance coalesce here, a mash-up of chic and cheap.

DURING THE DAY, THE INTERSECTION BUZZES LIKE A HIVE, AS COLORFUL as an aquarium of gaudy fish. Passing by are bargain hunters, college students, commuters, tourists, teens hanging out with other teens, and the occasional street photographer. Lawyers and accountants cross paths with homeless men clutching lumpy garbage bags. Windows of the office buildings and condos glimmer like unseeing eyes, reflecting shades of tan and steely gray from construction barely a decade old. Nearby is Chinatown, with its buffet of Asian cuisine and culture. At night the neon necklace of the Paramount Theater bathes faces of showgoers in shades of orange and rose.

But imagine this: What if, in the space of two days, everything in Downtown Crossing and the blocks around it disappeared? The department stores, the restaurants, the theaters, the condos, the offices . . . the people. Gone. Just gone. What if you emerged from the subway into what appeared to be a nuclear wasteland? Swaths of twisted wreckage, granite snapped into pieces like china, bricks piled as carelessly as if a young giant built a sandcastle and gleefully knocked it down. Among the ruined

THE FIRE FIEND!

Terrible Conflagration in Boston!

FEARFUL BLOW TO THE BUSINESS INTERESTS OF THE CITY!

The Most Costly and Valuable Warehouses and Mercantile Establishments Laid in Ashes!

THE LOSS ESTIMATED BY MILLIONS !

The Calamity Attended by Loss of Life!

THE STARTING POINT ON SUMMER STREET.

Uncontrollable Progress of the Flames !

THE FIREMEN POWERLESS TO SAVE.

A Tornado Created by the Intense Heat.

FLAMES AND SPARKS BLOWN IN ALL DIRECTIONS.

Buildings Lapped Up by the Flames and Reduced to Ashes in a Moment.

"TING SCENES IN THE "REETS.

A headline in the *Boston Sunday Herald* of November 10, 1872, details the ferocity of the Fire Fiend.

streets are odd bits of buildings, arches rising like ruins of the Roman Empire, the stripped-down bones of once-elegant structures, leaving no hint of the furnishing and merchandise once housed inside.

Imagine that this devastation goes on for blocks to the northeast, reaching Franklin, Devonshire, Federal, Congress, and Pearl Streets, and stretching over High and Purchase Streets, covering a half mile to Boston Harbor, where an uncaring tide laps the charred posts of once-bustling wharves.

We are imagining no mere fire. This is scorched-earth havoc, a kind of destruction that, to modern eyes, recalls Hiroshima or Dresden. The common term for this kind of fire is *conflagration*—a word firefighters use to describe a fire so hot that it can ignite material across natural or man-made barriers, such as a street. You could also call it a firestorm, a fire that creates its own wind, becoming a small hurricane of sparks and smoke. But let's use the epithet the politicians, pundits, and reporters used so lavishly and liberally at the time as they tried to fathom the devastation: the "Fire Fiend."

From November 9 to 11, 1872, the Fire Fiend ruled Boston. Igniting in a building at the corner of Kingston and Summer Streets, fire rampaged through the downtown, scorching nearly sixty-five acres and obliterating 776 buildings. A quickly overwhelmed Boston fire force called for help and fire companies from the surrounding communities, plus Connecticut, New Hampshire, and Maine, rushed in, bringing in fire engines by train as needed.

This can't be called Boston's worst fire. That dubious distinction likely belongs to the 1942 Cocoanut Grove nightclub fire, which resulted in the deaths of nearly five hundred people. But the Fire Fiend was the largest and most expensive fire in the history of Boston, a city that has seen more than its share of brutal fires. The Fire Fiend took out warehouses, factories, stores, and apartments. It destroyed the Trinity Church and two newspaper offices. It nearly destroyed the Old South Meeting House and burned to within three blocks of City Hall. It left thousands homeless or out of work and some financially ruined. The assessed value of the destroyed properties was nearly $13.5 million and personal property loss totaled $60 million—equal to $1.6 billion today.

An illustration in the November 30, 1872, *Harper's Weekly* captured the devastation of the Great Boston Fire. This shows the scene of the ruins from the west side of Washington Street. The Old South Meeting House and the ruins of the Transcript building are in the foreground.

At least eleven firefighters and one former firefighter died fighting the fire. The total number of deaths is difficult to determine, which was not uncommon in large fires of the day, but likely totaled twenty to twenty-five, including firefighters. That the toll was not higher is surprising, given not only the extent of the destruction, but also the crowds of people who packed the fiery streets to retrieve property or watch the mesmerizing Fiend rising over the skyline.

Bostonians witnessed their city burn with horrified awe. In her diary, *Little Women* author Louisa May Alcott called the fire a "very splendid and terrible sight." Oliver Wendell Holmes Sr., the famed poet and physician, saw the fire "dissolve the great high buildings which seem to melt away in it." Eighteen-year-old Grace Linzee Revere, a great-granddaughter of Paul Revere, said the flames appeared to roll up to meet the sky, saying, "The moon was directly over them, and it really seemed as though the flames were running a race to burn it up." Abolitionist William Lloyd Garrison found it "a sad, wonderful and fascinating sight to see the ruins from Washington Street, extending from Summer to Milk Streets, thus sweeping broadly to the water." Even the city's best writers said words failed them when they tried to recount what they saw.

The Fire Fiend was finally halted by a concerted effort involving firefighters from across New England. Boston reeled and the nation mourned. The Bangor, Maine, *Whig & Courier* told the entire story in a single dramatically stacked headline:

Boston in Flames!
Fearful Conflagration
The Heart of the City Burned Out!
The Fire Spreads in All Directions!
FANNED BY A FIERCE GALE
Buildings Blown Up to Save the City
Frightful Devastation!
THE GREAT WHOLESALE BLOCKS DESTROYED
The Flames Finally Checked!!
Boundary of the Ruins

SEVENTY ACRES BURNED OVER!!
Losses $80,000 to $90,000,000

Perhaps the most telling of all declarations was this label repeated in newspapers around the world: "SECOND CHICAGO."

Because the country had seen this before, just a year before, in fact. Reporters simply dusted off the hyperboles of October 1871 and plastered them in new configurations of newsprint type.

You know about the Chicago Fire? Of course, you do. Let's sing it together, like you probably did at camp:

> Late last night, when we were all in bed,
> Mrs. O'Leary left a lantern in the shed.
> And when the cow kicked it over,
> She winked her eye and said,
> It'll be a hot time in the old town tonight!
> FIRE, FIRE, FIRE!

From October 8 to 10, 1871, a conflagration consumed two-thirds of the city of Chicago, burning 2,000 acres and destroying 17,500 buildings. An estimated three hundred people lost their lives. Supposedly the fire started when a cow kicked over a lantern. That tale is doubtful, but the myth remains powerful, underscoring an unsettling truth that devastation can result from a single careless event.

Certainly, fires have always been a menace to human civilization. Think of the Great London Fire of 1666 and, centuries later, the earthquake-induced fire of 1908 in San Francisco, perhaps the worst in this country's history. The mid-nineteenth century in America was a period of particularly acute destruction. The country's rapid urban growth ushered in an era of unprecedented fire losses, when the nation's cities were in danger of burning down.

"California and New York were like giant andirons flanking an entire nation that threatened to go up in smoke," authors Margaret and Robert Hazen note in their book, *Keepers of the Flame*. "Although the devastation can be measured in many different ways, almost every conventional yardstick reveals a country plagued by what one early twentieth-century publication called 'Enormous Fire Losses . . .'" The yardstick for the Chicago Fire of 1871 "reached epic proportions." (It's worth noting that the Peshtigo forest fire in northeastern Wisconsin occurred the day the Chicago Fire started, killing more than a thousand people.)

Whether sparked by a startled bovine or another cause, the Chicago Fire was an epic conflagration, spreading uncontrollably through dry wooden structures with tar and shingle roofs to the shores of Lake Michigan. News of the fire sent a shudder through urban firefighters around the US, including the chief of the Boston Fire Department, John S. Damrell.

Those who study the Great Boston Fire will almost invariably find themselves intrigued by the character of Damrell. Fire chiefs in those days were called "Chief Engineers," a reflection of how fire companies were then centered around and dependent on steam fire engines—contraptions that used, ironically enough, fire—to create pressure for streams of water that made firefighting more effective. As Paul A. Christian, Boston Fire Commissioner and Chief from 2000 to 2006 put it, Damrell was "a firefighter's firefighter," judicious, intelligent, and completely devoted to his profession, which then, as now, is a calling that engenders fierce devotion and commitment from generations of men and women.

Even as Chicago's streets cooled, Damrell boarded a train for Illinois to spend a few days reviewing the damage. He met with General Philip Sheridan, the Civil War hero stationed in Chicago, who played a significant role directing firefighting efforts. What Damrell learned surely chilled him. Before traveling to the Windy City, he knew Boston's growth had far outstripped its firefighters' ability to keep the city safe. Now, he believed, time was running out. He returned from Chicago and redoubled his efforts to convince Boston city officials that they were sitting on a tinderbox. While he was able to bring about some improvements, such as the construction of a special fire boat, most of his recommendations were ignored.

This, then, is the real issue of the Great Boston Fire. All that destruction was a disaster foretold, a tragedy caused not by capricious nature or an unfathomable deity, but by the determined ignorance of men who, like far too many figures in history, supposed nothing would go wrong. It is a lesson in hubris and in the courage of those who doggedly, determinedly,

BOSTON IN FLAMES.

A popular lithograph of the Great Boston Fire shows its fiery force. AUTHOR'S COLLECTION

do what they know is right despite criticism and disgrace. What is truly remarkable about Damrell is what happened to him after the fire, when he was largely blamed for the destruction. A lesser man might have licked his wounds in seclusion, but Damrell never stopped pushing the lessons of the Great Fire: that both prevention and vigilance are the chief enemies of the Fire Fiend.

This is not the first time I have written about the Great Boston Fire. I included a chapter about it in my first book, *Boston on Fire: A History of Fires and Firefighting in Boston*. The fire has also been the subject of various books, most written in haste after the fire, and numerous articles. It was the focus of a 1972 special magazine section of the *Boston Globe* to mark the one-hundredth anniversary of the fire.

So, what is there left to say?

Well, plenty.

When I wrote my chapter on the Great Boston Fire in 2002, I did not have access to the records, documents, and other resources now available via the Internet, which has let me write a better, more systematic examination of the fire, its context, and its aftermath. Since *Boston on Fire* was published, a former computer entrepreneur, Bruce Twickler, wrote, directed, and produced a remarkable documentary, "Damrell's Fire: How One Firefighter Stopped America's Cities from Burning Down." Twickler and crew built a computer model of 1872 Boston and then "burned" it through digital wizardry. In the spirit of academic altruism, Twickler also uploaded much primary source material to the web, the beginning of what would become a trove of material on the fire hitherto only available in physical archives. Over the years, I've run across other primary source material in online archives and, surprisingly, on eBay.

I've wanted to return to the scene of the fire because the disaster was more than a huge conflagration. Other themes and stories branch out from the main narrative in ironic twisting streams. I've learned how the Fire Fiend turned out to be a source of entertainment, as odd as that seems. Images of ruined Boston became a mini-industry for the day's photographers and illustrators. While no photographs of the actual fire have ever been found, and likely none exist, Boston photographers swarmed the so-called Burnt District after the flames cooled. Many of the photos they took were processed into stereoscopes, a popular parlor game of the day, in which photos are viewed through a special lens for a 3D effect—Victorian-era special effects.

There is another, even more important reason for this book. The Chicago Fire and the tale of Mrs. O'Leary's cow are instantly recognizable as Americana. The city's professional soccer team is called Chicago Fire, and a search on Amazon will yield dozens of books about the Chicago disaster—a good portion of them for children. But the current generation of Bostonians knows virtually nothing of the Great Boston Fire. What you hold in your hand is the first systematic, sourced, print account of the fire in fifty years that also includes a social history of its cause and effect. Boston firefighters—and fire buffs in general, most prominently the members of the Box 52 Association—are familiar with the fire, along with a smattering of historians, architects, and city planners. The vast majority of those passing daily through Downtown Crossing have no clue about the drama that occurred there nearly 150 years ago. They don't know they are walking streets built on ash.

The past, as William Faulkner tells us, is never really dead; it's not even past. As I began this book, massive bushfires, fueled by global warming, swept through Australia. In the US, the Camp Fire wiped out the town of Paradise, California, and brutal forest fires returned the next year. The Fire Fiend has not disappeared; it's just taken other forms.

There are modern Damrells. Young Swedish climate activist Greta Thunberg has endured ridicule to declare that our house—the earth—is on fire and that we must rush to the rescue. And then there was the Covid-19 pandemic. In late 2019, a Chinese physician, Dr. Li Wenliang, attempted to warn Wuhan-area hospitals about the spread of a deadly new virus; he was instructed by police to keep his concerns to himself. He later succumbed to Covid-19, among the first of the millions who died worldwide. In the US, just a year earlier, the Trump administration reduced funding for the Centers for Disease Control and Prevention's pandemic-response programs as part of an overall cost-cutting move. And while Dr. Anthony Fauci, chief of the Laboratory of Immunoregulation, eventually became a kind of folk hero for his role, early in the pandemic, his comments were met with hostility by many politicians, including, at times, the US President. As the coronavirus began its march around the globe, many denied that it was worse than the typical flu, or that wearing masks could minimize its spread, or that it even existed at all.

We still refuse to listen to those who warn of possibilities and consequence: the whistleblowers, the Cassandras, the prophets of doom. "Don't magnify the situation so much," we say. "What do you know anyway? It can't happen here. Don't tell me to wear a mask against my will. Lighten up."

Boston didn't listen to John S. Damrell, a man who tried to tell the city that it faced a monumental disaster, and who first bore the brunt of the blame for what happened. He would understand the dilemma of those who warn us of the unimaginable, and whom we ignore until a strange light wakes us from sleep and we open the door to a furnace.

Note on use of firefighter/firemen: Women have joined the fire service in increasing numbers and the proper title for everyone in the service today is "firefighter." In the nineteenth century, those in the service were all men, so I use both the term "firemen" and "firefighter" in the context of the 1872 fire.

CHAPTER 1

Hubris in the Hub

Boston is just like other places of its size;—only, perhaps, consider-
ing its excellent fish-market, paid fire-department, superior monthly
publications, and correct habit of spelling the English language, it has
some right to look down on the mob of cities.
—OLIVER WENDELL HOLMES SR.
THE AUTOCRAT OF THE BREAKFAST-TABLE, APRIL 1858

OLIVER WENDELL HOLMES SR., THE PHYSICIAN, POET, INVENTOR, AND
father of a future Supreme Court Justice, was the epitome of a Victorian-
era Bostonian: brilliant, self-important, and subject to social bias. He contributed much to the reputation of his hometown, not least of which was
a nickname for which newspaper headline writers have been eternally
grateful—his tongue-in-cheek reference to the gold-domed Massachusetts State House as the "Hub of the Solar System." The "Hub" has been
shorthand for Boston ever since.

In 1872 the Hub was a city of about 250,000, with a growing population of immigrants, particularly from Ireland. A busy port city, with ships
from England and Europe docking at the harbor's many wharves, the
Hub was a capital of commerce, a center for the sale and export of wholesale goods. The city jealously guarded its position as the springboard for
the American Revolution, and its wealthy families, the Brahmins, considered it a guardian of culture, the "Athens of America." Reformers supported causes ranging from temperance to women's suffrage to animal
welfare. The city nurtured writers, poets, and intellectual elites such as
Henry Wadsworth Longfellow, Ralph Waldo Emerson, William Ellery

Oliver Wendell Holmes Sr. epitomized Boston's intellectual elite.

Channing, and Louisa May Alcott—and others, even those without three names.

William Lloyd Garrison, the passionate abolitionist, published his influential newspaper *The Liberator* in Boston beginning in 1831 while living on bread and water and sleeping on the floor of the paper's office in Merchants Hall at the corner of Congress and Water Streets. The aging warrior, who had riled many moderate abolitionists for his uncompromising stance on slavery, continued to live in Boston in the 1870s, taking a lively interest in the politics of the day, including advocacy for better treatment for Black Americans. Writing was a valued skill; young and old kept journals or wrote letters on a daily basis. Bostonians flocked to the theater, listened to lectures and sermons, and read magazines such as the Boston-based *Atlantic Monthly*, the national *Harper's Weekly* (with its sumptuous illustrations of world events), and "ladies' journals" such as *American Homes*, which published a mix of fiction and household tips. In this era, Boston didn't walk as much as swagger, says Stephen Puleo, author of *A City So Grand: The Rise of an American Metropolis, Boston 1850-1900.* "It was a city on the move."

In 1872, Boston was still descending from a cloud of fervent civic pride, due to the National Peace Jubilee, a massive series of concerts and performances meant to celebrate the end of the Civil War. A high point in the five-day event, held from June 15 to 19, 1869, was a performance of the Anvil Chorus from Verdi's *Il Trovalore* with a hundred Boston firemen who pounded hammers on anvils to create a melodious cacophony that, according to *American Heritage* magazine, "turned an Italian opera into an even greater showstopper as an American patriotic hymn." The jubilee appeared to be exactly what America needed as it closed out the 1860s, Puleo writes, "It was emotionally uplifting for a nation that had started the decade ripped apart by war and it was culturally important for a country and a city whose dedication to the arts was still questioned by Europe."

Amid the celebration of arts and culture, Boston was enjoying the latest Victorian technology and infrastructure. Lights in the city's residences and businesses, for example, were lit by gas from a network of pipes, which replaced lanterns and candles. Railroads linked the Hub to cities in the

WILLIAM LLOYD GARRISON.

An illustrated portrait of William Lloyd Garrison from an article about him in *Harper's Weekly*, June 14, 1879.

South and the West. Other innovations, such as the steam engine and a telegraph-based alarm system, had greatly improved firefighting, easing the danger that had plagued Boston since its founding. Boston was so prone to fires that many declared it "was built to burn."

Generations of Boston youngsters would be awed by the sight of a steam fire engine, already lit and smoking, careening down the road drawn by a team of horses, as firemen raced to a blaze. The steam fire engine was, in fact, an ingenious contraption. Before its use, Boston fire companies responded to alarms by dragging a hand-powered pumper to a fire scene and plugging hoses into the nearest a water source, such as a reservoir or hydrant. With sheer brawn and a fierce sense of honor, groups of firemen grabbed the handles of these machines and pumped, creating pressure that would force streams of water on to a fire. This was far more effective than the bucket brigades of the past. It was an honor to "run with the masheens," as it was then called, although fire companies sometimes fought over who would get the distinction of being the first to plug into a hydrant and get water onto the fire.

Invented in the early 1800s, steam fire engines used "fire to fight fire" by burning coal or wood to generate energy and create water pressure. When plugged into a water source, these engines could shoot water through long leather hoses to rain streams on fire from the top down, the most efficient way to quell a blaze. Boston got its first steam engine, the *Miles Greenwood*, in 1854, and by 1860, the department had converted entirely to steam engines. These engines weighed from 6,800 to 10,500 pounds each, including about 450 feet of hose, and could throw from 300 to 550 gallons of water a minute to a horizontal distance of 320 feet and a vertical distance of 220 feet, then considered an amazing feat of technology. Horses had to be employed to pull this heavy machinery, and, after some grumbling about newfangled changes, steam engines and horses were accepted by the city's firemen. Horses were specially trained for fire work. They would be quickly harnessed to the engines after an alarm was struck, the engine fires would be lit, firemen would jump on, and the steeds would take off at a gallop. By 1872, Boston had a fleet of steam fire engines made by Hunneman, which was based in Boston, and Amoskeag, based in New Hampshire.

During the era of the hand-pumped fire engine, fire companies often staged competition to see who could produce the highest streams as shown in this illustration of an event on the Boston Common, from the May 10, 1851, *Gleason's Pictorial Drawing Room Companion*.

To modern eyes, the steam fire engine with its hodgepodge of a smokestack, bulbous boiler, twisting pipes, nozzles, gauges, and flywheel, may seem like a steampunk dream, but these were reliable, hard-working, and efficacious machines. Former Boston Fire Chief and Commissioner Paul Christian spoke highly of their effectiveness. "They worked great," he told me. The 1872 fire would test their limits.

The invention of the telegraph in the 1830s produced another uniquely Boston contribution to fire safely. Inspired by Samuel Morse's revolutionary invention, a telegraph fire-alarm system was conceived in 1850 and subsequently installed in 1852 by William Frances Channing (son of the prominent theologian William Ellery Channing) and engineer Moses Farmer, who would later work with Alexander Graham Bell on another signature invention. The fire alarm system, which drew on the principles of the electric telegraph, alerted firefighters as to the location and ferocity of a fire. Previously, the main option was to run through the streets, screaming, "Fire! Fire!"—a practice known as "hallooing fire"—and hope that word reached a firehouse or someone who could ring church bells to raise the alarm. The new alert system was the forerunner of today's first-responder technology. The city was crisscrossed with lines connecting hundreds of alarm boxes to a central headquarters atop Boston City Hall on School Street. When someone cranked a mechanism inside a box, it sent a signal to the headquarters. The man on duty noted the box's location and triggered instruments that rang bells throughout the city and in the firehouses.

For example, if the crank was turned in Box 52, located at the intersection of Summer and Bedford Streets, the bells would chime five times, then pause, then chime two more times. This signal would be repeated twice at an interval of a minute. Via a system of "running cards," firemen would know whether their company should respond to a fire reported in the area of Box 52. For a serious fire, a second alarm (ten rings, or "blows") would call in more fire companies and a third alarm (twelve blows twice) would call in even more. A fourth alarm (twelve blows three times) called in the entire department.

This system had one serious flaw. Due to the fear of miscreants triggering false alarms, alarm boxes were kept locked. Policemen had keys, as did nearby shopkeepers or residents—those designated as responsible people. This could cause delays, as those "hallooing fire" had to find a keyholder to open the box to send the alarm.

Even with the latest in technology, Boston was vulnerable to fire—nowhere more so than in its downtown commercial district, formerly a neighborhood for wealthy residents. Benjamin Franklin spent his young years there before departing for Philadelphia. Summer Street was once considered one of the city's most splendid avenues, with fine houses and huge trees overarching the street. Summer Street was home to the venerable Trinity Church, an Episcopal congregation dating to 1735 and, at the time of the fire, overseen by the Reverend Phillip Brooks, then one of the nation's best-known religious thinkers. (Brooks is remembered today for writing the lyrics to the Christmas carol "O Little Town of Bethlehem.") His flock had been moving out of the downtown to the Back Bay and other areas, so Brooks was now supervising the building of a new Trinity Church, an even more magnificent structure designed by the famed architect Henry Hobson Richardson, in Copley Square, about a mile away from Summer Street. In the years after the Civil War, the aristocratic mansions were demolished, and, according to Charles "Carleton" Coffin, a contemporary historian with a flair for overstatement, "In their places had risen magnificent palaces of trade, until every street in the district was flanked by the most substantial and architecturally beautiful edifices on this continent, if not in the world."

Hyperbole aside, the new construction in the area was truly more than utilitarian; structures were meant to be temples paying homage to the burgeoning forces of industry, capitalism, and commerce. They abounded with architectural frills and flourishes; they were made of brick and iron and faced with gleaming granite. Stately buildings housed retail and wholesale businesses for clothing, boots, shoes, leather, wool, and other dry goods; massive warehouses stored bundles and boxes of merchandise ready for shipment. Small factories with rows of sewing machines churned out women's clothing, such as the popular hoop skirts and bustles, and employed hundreds of women. Due to the development of steam-powered elevators, larger buildings could accommodate goods on higher floors; hence, buildings rose to hitherto impossible heights—four, five, and even six stories. The six-story Beebe Block, the prize of the commercial district housing some of the city's largest wholesale dealers, took up a large swath of Winthrop Square. "The effort was to cover the territory as closely as possible, and then to build stores upon it as high into the heavens," Diane Tarmy Rudnick wrote in her landmark 1971 dissertation on the political and economic forces that shaped Boston before and after the Great Fire, *Boston and the Great Fire of 1872: The Stillborn Phoenix*.

Boston was then the nation's publishing capital. Several leading publishers were in the downtown area, along with many of the city's

FRANKLIN STREET BEFORE THE FIRE

A view of Franklin Street in the heart of Boston's elegant commercial district before the fire. Source: *Boston Illustrated*, a pamphlet published by James R. Osgood & Co.

half-dozen newspapers, including the *Boston Transcript* and the upstart *Boston Globe*. A few blocks from Trinity Church was the popular C. F. Hovey's department store, a business founded by the forward-thinking Charles Fox Hovey, who pioneered the then-unusual concept of fixed prices for customers (he didn't want them to have to haggle with clerks) and profit-sharing for his employees. The downtown had some homes and boarding houses. But the city's poorer citizens, including recent immigrants, packed into a hilly section to the north known as Fort Hill, once an area for fine residential homes but, by the 1870s, considered a slum. In 1872, it was gradually being leveled for new development.

Many new buildings were topped with something called a Mansard roof, a popular architectural feature in which the roof has two slopes on all four sides and the lower slope becomes steeper than the upper one. They were designed by French architect François Mansart who used the style for his Paris hotels and chateaus in the seventeenth century. Averaging twelve to twenty feet high, most Mansard roofs in Boston were made of wood such as pine and coated with tar.

The Mansard roof faced a cadre of detractors. In a furious article in the November 25, 1871, *Boston Advertiser,* architectural gadfly Charles Bird of Watertown warned that the roofs were a fire hazard, a bonfire waiting for a spark. Architect A.C. Martin would later say a Mansard roof was not necessarily dangerous, but when constructed out of wood, as most in Boston were, rather than stone or copper, it could be "a very dangerous feature." Boston fire chief John Damrell would later call them "elevated lumber yards." This elegant feature, however, crowned Boston's status as a commercial realm of national importance. Even Damrell acknowledged the grandeur of the Hub's business section, saying, "These magnificent stories and massive warehouses were the pride of Boston merchants and architects."

The Hub thus had a decidedly mixed character in the nineteenth century: inventive, smug, high-minded, and materialistic. It was a place for shrewd businessmen and ethereal poets. It was a place where civic leaders could not wrap their heads around the possibility that their shining city on a hill was sitting on a tinderbox.

This was the city into which John S. Damrell was born.

CHAPTER 2

A Self-Reliant Man

The Chief Engineer of 1872 was a self-reliant man . . . with experience not only on the fire department but in the building trade and the field of politics.

—John Vahey, Boston District Fire Chief
"The Epizootic Fire"

I once fell in love with a nineteenth-century fire chief. While writing my first book on fires, I became infatuated with John Stanhope Damrell—pronounced DAM-rell—the hero (or perhaps the scapegoat) of the Great Fire of 1872.

I was hardly alone. Almost everyone who studies this conflagration falls hard for Damrell, none more so than filmmaker Bruce Twickler. In 2003, when Twickler made a documentary on the 1872 fire, he became so intrigued by Damrell that he ended up changing the title of his film from something generic about the disaster to "Damrell's Fire: How One Firefighter Stopped America's Cities from Burning Down." In Twickler's telling, Damrell became almost a kind of nineteenth-century Marvel superhero, complete with the special powers of foresight and the angst that accompanies insight.

It is easy to be enamored of a man who seemed to epitomize the better traits of the Victorian gentleman, to admire his sense of honor, duty, and initiative, and to overlook his streaks of stubborn self-righteousness. Still, an understanding of Damrell's actual personality remains elusive, and his very measured eloquence—as seen both in his speech and writing—tends to obscure what he might have been like in person. Photos

Boston Fire Chief John S. Damrell in a lithograph by E. R. Howe. COURTESY OF
THE BOSTON ATHENAEUM

and illustrations from the 1870s show a plain-faced man with mild eyes, receding sandy hair, and fashionable sideburns cruising along the side of his face. He sports a luxurious moustache that he (perhaps lovingly) cultivated all his life; as shown in later photos, it eventually grows to resemble a tall, untrimmed hedge. He was known to be blunt and dismissive with those who presumed to tell him how to fight a fire, but his eyes have more of a humorous twinkle than a fierce intensity. When I picture him, I think of him as having something of the brilliance and obstinance of the doctor in Henrik Ibsen's famous play, "An Enemy of the People," who tries to tell his town a truth that its citizens don't want to hear. Damrell was a bit shrewder than Ibsen's Dr. Thomas Stockmann; the Bostonian had a canny political side. If he had a major flaw, it might have been his misguided faith that if you lay out the facts, you will win the argument. His finest hours may not have been during the Great Fire itself, but in the long decades that followed.

Damrell's early life was marked with difficulties. He was born in Boston's North End neighborhood on June 28, 1828. The North End was one of the city's oldest sections; Paul Revere lived there and nearby was Copp's Hill, with its even-then ancient burial ground overlooking Boston Harbor. Twickler and his research team traced Damrell's lineage back to a group of English immigrants who settled in New England and worked as mariners and masons, printers and privateers, soldiers and coopers. His father, Samuel Edward Damrell, was born in 1807 in Newburyport, a fishing community north of Boston. He married Ann Stanhope in 1827; they settled in the North End and later moved to Cambridge. In 1835, Damrell's two-year-old sister died—childhood deaths were not uncommon—and then in December; his mother succumbed, likely to typhus. At the age of ten, the boy worked summers on a farm in the nearby town of Haverhill; perhaps his father wanted him to get away from unhealthy city air. When John was twelve, his father died, probably from tuberculosis. John was largely raised by his uncle Thomas Damrell.

Just two years after his father's death, John left school at age fourteen (his later remarks indicated this action was not voluntary) and became an apprentice to the master builder and architect Isaac Melvin of Cambridge. It's likely that the upheavals of his family life helped to make John resilient and self-reliant, and he showed an aptitude for carpentry and construction that would stay with him the rest of his life. As an apprentice, he learned how to make boy's sleds and would bring them from Cambridge to Boston and sell them for a good profit. On April 11, 1850, Damrell married Susan Emily Hill of Cambridge, the sister of Elvira Hill Damrell, who had married his uncle Thomas (and who may have also been briefly married to his father after his mother died.) John and Susan Damrell had five children; two daughters died young and a third died at twenty-two. His two sons survived into late adulthood. Damrell eventually moved his family to Boston and by 1856 he launched a building partnership, which he would run for decades.

At age eighteen, John found another activity that, we might speculate, linked him to his late father and even gave him a sense of family: firefighting. His father had served as a volunteer firefighter, and his uncle Thomas and a cousin were also volunteers. John began to volunteer as well. It became quickly apparent to his fellow firefighters in the "Hero" company, or Engine Company 6, that young John was a natural leader and instinctual firefighter. He knew how buildings were put together, giving him insight into the forces that might tear them apart. He was later part of Engine Company 4, dubbed the Cataract. In 1853, his fellow Cataract firefighters elected him clerk of the company; by the next year, he was elected assistant foreman and then foreman in 1855. On July 4, 1856, his colleagues presented him with a solid-silver trumpet—the trumpet is a symbol of the fire service.

Firefighting has always been a fraternity, a calling for men and later women who considered it an honor to put life and limb on the line for others. Alfred Downes, a fire history author and New York City Fire Department Secretary, reflected the reverence that many held for firefighters when he wrote in 1907, "One and all, enginemen and hook-and-ladder men, they stand shoulder to shoulder fighting fiercely and fearlessly to subdue the flames and protect property and to save human life. . . . They are guardians of modern life and they are also among the heroes of modern romance." Firefighters had a fierce sense of camaraderie for their companies and for their profession. They knew they were a bulwark against the scourge of fire, which could wipe out a family or a

Engine Company 4, the Cataract, continues to pump water on the still smoking ruins of the 1872 fire days later as shown in this photo by James Wallace Black.
BOSTON PUBLIC LIBRARY

fortune in a few minutes. As the authors of the *Keepers of the Flame* put it, "As a group, [firefighters] gave the impression that they had extraordinary powers and that impression, illusion thought it might have been, helped to bolster the public's confidence that they might, eventually, gain control over the destructive aspects of fire."

While firefighters in the nineteenth century needed tenacity and guts, they also had to acquire technical acumen as well. Over the decades, fire departments morphed from all-volunteer units into a mix of permanent, on-call, and volunteer personnel. Supervisors had to know how to run and maintain the hand-pumpers and, later, the steam engines. That's why the fire chief was called the chief engineer and the assistant fire chiefs were known as assistant engineers. Via on-the-job training and mentorships, firefighters learned to attack a fire: how to deploy the machinery, direct the streams, climb ladders to direct streams of water from great heights, and rescue civilians from burning buildings.

This fanciful cover from *Harper's Weekly* of February 8, 1873, captures the popular perception of the heroic fireman. Note the trumpet hanging from his arm.

Damrell excelled in these areas. In 1858 he became an assistant engineer, a position he held for the next ten years. Expertise alone, however, was not what projected him to the position of chief engineer in 1866. Damrell also had political chops. In 1857 he took time off from the fire department to be elected to the city Common Council. At that time, Boston's municipal government consisted of a Board of Aldermen of twelve members elected at large and a Common Council of sixty-four members elected four from each ward.

Together, the two bodies were referred to as the City Council. Damrell only served in office for one year, but he racked up other civic experience. During the Civil War, he oversaw a committee for Ward Six that recruited soldiers for the North's war effort and received the military title of Captain. He was a Mason of the 32nd degree, and a member of the Knights of Honor, the Royal Arcanum, the Odd Fellows, and the Good Templars. In other words, while he lacked higher education and could not be considered part of Boston's Brahmin elite, he was as well connected as any businessman in the city. This became apparent in 1866, when he ran for the position of head of the Boston Fire Department. The chief engineer was elected by the Board of Aldermen, and Damrell's election, according to Boston fire historian Arthur Brayley, was "one of the most exciting local struggles in the history of the department, or that ever occupied the attention of the City Council."

At that time, the Boston Fire Department was considered a national model because of the professional quality of its firemen. However, it had a convoluted organizational structure. The mayor annually appointed an eight-member Joint Standing Committee on the Fire Department that included three members from the Board of Aldermen, and five from the Common Council. Assistant engineers were elected annually by the City Council; in 1872, there were fourteen who oversaw the city's eight fire districts. The city also had a joint committee on fire alarms, a superintendent of fire alarms, and another joint committee for purchasing land and erecting and repairing station houses. The city's water board located and controlled hydrants and reservoirs. "It would hardly be possible to devise a more ingenious scheme for dividing responsibility, and insuring the largest possible outlay than that adopted by the City Council for the government of the fire department," James K. Bugbee observed in 1873 in the *North American Review*

The rank and file of the city's 459 firemen were divided into forty-two companies: twenty-one steam engine companies, eleven hose companies (which carried extra hose to fire scenes), seven ladder companies, and three extinguisher wagons that worked a bit like fire extinguishers today. These used chemicals to create water pressure that would allow firemen to quickly get water on a fire. Each company had both a number and a name, the latter either a colorful moniker like Mazeppa, Maverick, Torrent, Independence, Barnicoat, Protector, and Eagle, or a name, such as T.C. Amory and Elisha Smith. In 1867 Engine Company 11, based on Sumner Street in East Boston, was named the John S. Damrell in honor of the new chief. Much of what is now Boston today was then divided into different towns. Gradually these communities were annexed by the large city. By 1872 Roxbury and Dorchester had been annexed to the city and their fire companies were now part of Boston.

"EAGLE" Steam Fire Engine, No. 3, Boston Fire Department.

In the 1870s, each Boston fire company had both a name and a number. Here Engine Company 3, the Eagle, is depicted on its way to a fire, its steam engine already lit and smoking. Source: W. F. Chandler and Co.'s *Chandler & Co.'s full account of the great fire in Boston and the ruins*

One issue that would bother Damrell and play a part in subsequent events was the lack of firehouses in the older downtown area that had become the commercial district. This area, known as "Boston Proper," had just six steam fire engines, six hose companies, and two ladder companies. Yet this area's value was assessed at a whopping $514,697,450, while an outlying area, assessed at only $31,395,300, also had six steam fire engines. While Boston civic leaders were known to be tight with a dollar, the city considered its fire service worth a substantial investment. By 1870 the city was spending more than $450,000 annually on fire salaries, equipment, water costs and other expenses, about 4 percent of total municipal expenditures. In 1872 Damrell was paid $3,300 a year. Assistant engineers made $500 a year, while enginemen, drivers, and foremen made between $3.00 and $3.25 a day. Boston's fire department cost more per capita than any other major American city, although the city's expenses per fireman were well below those of Philadelphia and New York; the city reported a lower level of losses from fire than either New York or Philadelphia. The late nineteenth century was a time when cities nationwide began to experience huge losses by fire; urban conflagrations showed a fairly steady evolution to ever more destructive and costly incidents.

Resourceful, hardworking, and skillful, Damrell nonetheless seemed to have a singular flaw. A modest man, not given to hyperbole, he believed he could successfully negotiate funding requests by making sober, reasonable arguments. He appeared to be impatient with wealthy Brahmins who had never soiled their hands with manual labor yet told him how to do his job. As someone who had been born in humble circumstances and raised himself to prosperity, he was judicious in his spending. He would hesitate to recommend anything not absolutely needed for public safety, and he expected the responses to his recommendations to be as thoughtful as his own approach. If only he could lay out the facts and particulars of a dangerous situation, those who held the purse strings in the city government would respond. He would learn that arguments, however carefully stated, may not sway those who believed they had their own facts.

By October 1871, the forty-three-year-old Damrell had a profitable building and carpentry business, a spacious home on Beacon Hill that housed his extended family, and the prestigious, if often difficult, position of Boston's top fireman. The 1870 census showed he had assets of $55,000; he could be considered a wealthy man. And even though Boston had suffered an unusually large number of fires in the past few years, the quick and efficient work of Boston firefighters prevented any major conflagrations. Still, Damrell continued to push for multiple improvements in the fire service. He pressed city officials about issues such as water pressure, hydrants, and additional stations and equipment, even when repeatedly rebuffed.

And then came the Chicago fire. Surely after this, they would listen to him.

CHAPTER 3

A Hot Time in the Old Town

It is an unpleasant thing for an Engineer of the Fire Department—
when we have a committee that [doesn't] see fit to endorse his recom-
mendations—to push it over their heads.

—JOHN DAMRELL
TESTIMONY IN THE REPORT OF THE COMMISSIONERS
APPOINTED TO INVESTIGATE THE CAUSE AND
MANAGEMENT OF THE GREAT FIRE IN BOSTON

THE NEWS FROM CHICAGO IN OCTOBER 1871 SHOCKED MANY AMERI-
cans, including an aging activist who took a fire buff's interest in huge
conflagrations. "That grand and prosperous city has had reduced to ashes
all its magnificent hotels, warehouses, churches, elevators, railroad depots,
private residences, &c., &c. leaving only the outskirts at hundreds of millions of dollars and the number of homeless and penniless persons at
least one hundred thousand," William Lloyd Garrison lamented in an
October 11, 1871, letter to his daughter Fanny. "Such a terrible scene was
scarcely ever before witnessed under the sun; and the amount of suffering
and agony, of bereavement and horror no tongue or pen can depict."

For two days, from October 8 to 10, a conflagration swept through the
City of Big Shoulders, leaving more than two thousand acres scorched,
seventeen thousand buildings destroyed, one hundred thousand people
homeless, and an estimated three hundred dead. Damage was estimated
to exceed $200 million. The fire spread four and a half miles from the
ignition point on the South Side of Chicago to Lake Michigan and to
the prairie, where it ended "only because there was nothing more to burn,"

Chicagoans flee into Lincoln Park to escape the Chicago Fire, as depicted in this illustration in *Harper's Weekly*, November 4, 1871.

said Charles F. Haywood in *General Alarm: A Dramatic Account of Fires and Firefighting in America*. Contributing to the conflagration's spread were a sustained drought, a delayed alarm, the proliferation of wooden structures (even the sidewalks in Chicago were made of wood), and a high wind from the south. A fire the previous night had also depleted the strength of the city's fire department. As Haywood put it, Chicago was "a very devil's brew."

One fire professional looked upon the destruction and saw not the unique factors that made it so terrible, but the threads that reached east to his own city. Boston Chief Engineer John S. Damrell arrived in Chicago on October 19 after a two-day train ride to view the destruction firsthand and deliver a generous financial donation from Boston and its firefighters to their counterparts in Chicago. He was shaken to his core by the experience.

The Chicago Fire "is, in my judgment, without a parallel in the history of the world," Damrell told city councilors of the Boston Fire Committee,

A Currier & Ives lithograph shows people fleeing across the Randolph Street Bridge during the Chicago Fire. CHICAGO HISTORICAL SOCIETY

which oversaw the fire department, on October 28, 1871. "It laid waste alike the dwellings of the poor, the palaces of the rich, magnificent store-houses with their millions of merchandise, hotels, public buildings, water-works, gas-works, the entire records of the county of Cook (both public and private), and drove 150,000 men, women and children upon the wide prairies, with the canopy of heaven as their only shelter, and mother earth as the only bosom upon which to rest their wearied limbs, placing the millionaire and the poorest mendicant of the city upon an equal footing."

Damrell had been charged with bringing money raised by Boston firemen to their Midwest brethren. On his return, he described in his report to city officials how he politely but shrewdly declined to give the $3,000 to any group but the firefighters themselves. "A long as I live, I shall never forget the scene that transpired as I handed . . . the munificent gift of the Boston Fire Department to the firemen of Chicago. The tears that rolled over their cheeks were far more expressive, more eloquent and touching than any words human lips can utter."

Damrell described the ruins of Chicago in the most lurid terms he could conjure: "Think, gentlemen, of a thickly settled city, with space of seven-eighths to a mile wide and five miles long swept of everything. The lime, cement, and in fact it would seem as if everything but the brick, stone, and iron itself consumed. The streets themselves are as clean as if they had been swept, the edge stones shivered with the heat and blown away.... The fire must have reached a white heat to have consumed everything as it did."

There was a method to the madness in the way Damrell depicted the disaster. He lathered on details like icing on a cake, hoping the Board of Aldermen would realize—as he did—that Boston was in real danger of experiencing a fire as devastating as that in Chicago. For years, he had warned about problems with water pressure and the numbers and locations of firehouses, hydrants, and new construction. Now, he believed, his warnings would finally be heeded.

Almost since his election as chief, Damrell had been warning about the lack of water—the first and primary tool of firefighting—in the city's congested business district. Boston had a long history of improving its water supply as the city grew. When first settled, the city depended on wells, rain barrels, and a spring on Boston Common. From 1795 to 1848, city water was drawn from Jamaica Pond, just south of the city proper, through wooden pipes. Beginning in 1848, Lake Cochituate, which was formed by damming a tributary of the Sudbury River west of Boston, became the main source of water for the city; water flowed fifteen miles to supply water mains running under the streets. About this time, with the introduction of hand-pumped fire engines, the fire department was restructured into a more professional organization that relied less on volunteers and more on paid employees who could maintain the "masheens," as the pumpers were called.

Water was used for drinking and firefighting. Hydrants connecting to the mains were installed at intervals along city blocks, much as they are today; as of 1872, about 2,606 had been placed throughout the city. Additionally, reservoirs, or cisterns, were built under the streets, fed by pipes from the regular water mains; firemen could also tap these for their steam fire engines. This system had proven adequate when the downtown was a residential area. Indeed, Boston's fire department developed a reputation as an effective, efficient service run by dedicated men.

By the 1860s, however, the downtown business district had developed into a densely packed commercial zone, with increasingly tall buildings chockablock on the narrow streets. Soon after he became fire chief, Damrell turned his focus to the six-inch water mains installed under the city streets and the four-inch pipes that connected the hydrants to the mains. The pipes were aging, and corrosion had likely reduced their diameters to as little as two-and-a-half inches. After some harrowing experiences when water ran low as firefighters battled blazes downtown, Damrell believed the mains and hydrants could no longer handle the water load for the pressure needed to reach the tops of the taller new buildings. He wanted to install eight-inch mains; this was vital for taking full advantage of the power of the steam fire engines. Older, hand-pumped machines drew only seventy-five gallons per minute, while steamers pumped at a rate of four hundred gallons per minute. Two steamers working on the same hydrant, or on hydrants near each other, might not draw enough water for either to produce a good stream. A vacuum caused by one steamer might leave none for the other. Moving fire engines to different hydrants took time and forced firemen to run long stretches of hose to bring streams closer to the flames.

The city then had two kinds of hydrants; the majority were of the type called the Boston hydrant. Damrell believed the other kind, the Lowry (sometimes spelled "Lowrey"), was more effective because it had four outlets, which allowed for the massing of several engines at one hydrant, whereas the Boston hydrant had only one outlet. The greater capacity of the Lowry hydrants meant that if they were connected to water main pipes of at least eight inches in diameter they would "give us a supply of water full equal, if not more than we now get from six of the ordinary hydrants," Damrell said in his annual report. Lowry hydrants had proven effective in a test in 1862 in Boston's Winthrop Square, and Damrell was also impressed with their use in Salem, Massachusetts. He wanted to switch to Lowry hydrants throughout the city, particularly in the commercial district downtown.

This was not Damrell's decision to make, however. He faced a ponderous bureaucracy; the Hub's water system, including the hydrants and reservoirs, were under the jurisdiction of the Boston Water Board. Soon after he became chief, Damrell had written directly to the president of the Water Board, a Mr. Thorndike, regarding his concerns about water. Thorndike did not respond. Instead, the president sent a clerk to Damrell saying that when they "were in want of any suggestions from the Chief Engineer of the Fire Department, he would let me know." Damrell swallowed this insult, but it stung. (Thorndike would later deny he made such a statement; Damrell would say he had witnesses.)

Clearly, the Water Board and the Fire Department were frequently at odds. This tension concerned city councilman William M. Flanders, a long-time member and former chairman of the Boston Fire Committee. Damrell brought Flanders on a visit to Franklin Street to point out where he thought hydrants should be placed, including one that he was anxious to keep near the building of *The Pilot*, Boston's Catholic newspaper (and which was later removed at the direction of the paper's publisher, Patrick Donahoe.) "If a fire should get in here and we should have a short supply of water, I don't think that any agency, human or divine, could stop it," Damrell told Flanders. Flanders was ready to listen. He was concerned that the fire department paid $60,000 to $70,000 annually for water from the city's water department but did not have jurisdiction over the hydrant placements—and that seemed unfair. Flanders was also concerned that the Water Board operated arbitrarily; it would frequently disable hydrants when repaving or changing sewage lines without notifying fire officials. "I don't think in a single instance did the Water Board notify the Fire Department that they had disturbed a hydrant," Flanders would later testify. He was particularly miffed about an incident in 1871, when the water was turned off at the firehouse for Engine Company Number Seven on East Street with no notification to anyone connected with the fire department. The firemen thought the water was frozen and inadvertently set the building on fire when they tried to thaw it out. "When [other] engines got down there, there was no water to play upon it. Whether there was any blame to be attached to anyone for that, I don't know," Flanders said.

Water was not Damrell's only issue. He also wanted more steam engines placed in the business district; 80 percent of the city's fires broke out in this area, and he didn't believe there was enough coverage. "We are constantly running into this district to do duty, instead of having the engines in the places where the fires are located," he would tell city councilors. The land there was, however, deemed too expensive to purchase for firehouses.

Damrell did not give up. In his annual reports of 1867, 1868, and 1869, as well as in a special report in 1868, Damrell tried to point out the various weak points in Boston's fire response: the water problems, the lack of apparatus, and the hydrants. He discovered city officials believed he was hired to do a job, not to tell them what should be done. When he brought up his concerns, he received a blunt response: "Don't try to magnify the wants of your department or of your office so much."

Why were Damrell's seemingly reasonable suggestions not seriously considered? Cost seems to have been the main objection. Harold Murdock, who researched the fire extensively for a paper read to the Bostonian Society on November 19, 1912, and who wrote an epistolary novel about the fire, concluded that "the hard-headed Yankee gentlemen who sat in the City Council were not farseeing and they abhorred extravagance," implying they believed that Damrell was exaggerating. In other words, it was Damrell's job to push for safety, but it was the job of the city and the water board to rein him back. Even the department's successes in fire management worked against the chief. Said Murdock: "The Boston public was complacent and inclined to regard all of our local institutions with pride and satisfaction."

In 1972 Charles Taylor, writing in a special *Boston Globe* anniversary supplement on the 1872 Boston fire, saw another force at work: the old-style politics of patronage and power that held sway in Boston's city government. "A system of annual appointments made everyone in the city government beholden and subservient," he wrote. While Taylor's analysis may have reflected more of the politics of the 1970s (when Boston was certainly awash in fighting over political fiefdoms), it's true that Damrell seemed to be unable to use his clout as a member of the city council—however brief his tenure there—to the fire department's advantage. His efforts may have been viewed as only attempting to promote his own fiefdom.

The local press played a part as well, as Damrell later recounted.

This proposition [for more firehouses] raised the cry of unnecessary and unqualified extravagance, the fire department was effective and efficient; and one of the leading journals replied in an editorial to the Chief Engineer as follows: "What matter to the city of Boston whether Hose Company No. 1 or Hose Company No. 100 should succeed in getting a stream of water on to Mrs. Muldoon's feather bed in advance of the other? This rival spirit of esprit de corps which seems to possess the rank and file of our department, is all right and proper; but when it seeks to entail upon the city such extravagant expenditure of money for the location of fire apparatus where the land could not be purchased at a less cost than fifty dollars per foot, to say nothing of the cost of erecting new buildings, it is highly absurd, and should meet the condemnation of every tax-paying citizen.

Treated as an annoying gadfly and a possible spendthrift, Damrell nevertheless persisted. His vision of effective firefighting stretched beyond the machinations of steam and water. He wanted to prevent fires from even breaking out. As a builder himself, he knew the tricks of the trade, the cost-cutting that might make a structure more susceptible to ignition and the materials that would make it more secure. He decried what he considered a "build-as-you-please" style in the city. In his very first report, he recommended that the city council adopt a system for inspecting unsafe buildings; the next year, the council gave him the power to appoint a building inspector. He chose former Chief Engineer George W. Bird for the post, but Bird had no legal authority; he could only appeal to the builders' good judgment.

Meanwhile, the burgeoning construction and the height of the buildings in the downtown section—and the popular Mansard roofs—continued to trouble Damrell. He convinced the city's insurance underwriters that they were running grave risks in insuring what passed as first-class property; largely for that reason, the city passed a new building code, Chapter 280 of the Acts of 1871, which gave the city the authority to establish a bureau of survey and inspection of new construction. Damrell had high hopes for the new code, even if he didn't think it went quite far enough.

The Chicago fire further galvanized Damrell. In his speech to the Fire Committee, he reiterated the need for an additional steam fire engine, to be stationed on Atlantic Avenue near the foot of State Street, to better protect the downtown. He also wanted a fire boat, or a "steam floating fire engine," to use water from the ocean to help protect the city's wharves. While acknowledging the commercial district's splendid architecture, he doubled down on describing the dangers of those Mansard roofs, saying that they had contributed to the destruction of Chicago as they caught fire and burned buildings from the top down. "I hope that our recently appointed Inspector of Buildings ... will vehemently urge, and not only urge, but demand, that all Mansard or French roofs shall be so finished as to afford us protection from any serious conflagration from that cause," he said.

Damrell did get his fire boat; it was under construction in November of 1872 and would go into service on January 1, 1873—two months after the Great Fire. Damrell's other concerns, however, went largely unheeded. Where Damrell saw similarities, others saw differences. Chicago was perceived as garish, insubstantial, inflammable, altogether lacking a sense of permanence, while Boston was intellectual, refined, and venerable. It was blessed with an excellent fire department with a dedicated, if annoying, chief and skilled engineers. What happened in the Windy City simply could not happen in the Hub of the Solar System.

CHAPTER 4

Black Beauty Down: The Horse Flu

By rail, by water, and by hoof, the Great Epizootic flowed through the North American urban network as if through blood vessels, revealing the intimate material interconnections among cities that tied their ecologies together. . . . Whether on the streets of Boston or the streets of New Orleans, horses powered the flow of goods and people within urban environments. They also biologically linked those environments to one another.

—SEAN KHERAJ
"THE GREAT EPIZOOTIC OF 1872–73"

THE SYMPTOMS BEGAN WITH A SORE THROAT, FOLLOWED BY A LOSS OF appetite, a hacking cough, harsh breathing, and a quickened pulse. Mucus began to drip from noses and yellowed eyes. Severe fatigue followed, with the inability to do even minor tasks such as running, walking, or pulling carts. For a week or more, those afflicted would be miserable, barely able to stand. After days of intense suffering, their eyes brightened, their noses stopped dripping. Rarely would they die. The horses generally recovered and returned to work.

An epidemic among animals, such as recent outbreaks of avian flu, is called an epizootic or panzootic. In what has become known as the Great Epizootic, horses in nearly every major urban center in the US and Canada fell ill, beginning in late September 1872. Before the mysterious disease fizzled out nearly a year later, transportation ground to a halt in city after city as horses fell sick.

This was no minor inconvenience. Horses pulled carts and wagons plus coaches, cabs, and multi-passenger trolleys. Trains connected cities, but within cities, people depended on horses for distances longer than a good walk. Goods transported by rail were pulled to their final destinations by horses. "With the horses too sick to work, streetcar companies suspended service, households lacked for milk, ice and groceries, saloons lacked for beer, work halted at construction sites, brickyards and factories, and undelivered freight accumulated at wharves and railroad depots," noted historian Ann N. Green. In city after city, business slowed to a standstill. The streets of New York fell silent. "Here and there great piles of merchandise had been massed and men were dragging up through narrow gangways fresh packages to add to the monumental piles," *Harper's Weekly* reported on November 16. Ox teams were brought in, cutting strange figures on city streets. A Springfield, Massachusetts, paper reported that in one barn, all sixty horses were sick and "such a coughing, wheezing and blowing of noses, no horseman had ever heard."

News reports traced the spread of the outbreak. On October 23, 1872, the *Boston Globe* reported the "horse disease" had afflicted most of the horses in Buffalo, New York, even though it was clear from subsequent reports that Boston's horses had already been infected as well. By October 25, "the plague" had spread so rapidly in Boston that "it can now, without exaggeration, be regarded as a great public misfortune," the *Globe* asserted.

A reporter from the *Boston Advertiser*, Sylvester Baxter, saw the remarkable spectacle of humans serving as draft animals. "Now and then a horsecar of the South Boston Street Railway hauled through Washington Street a gang of the company's drivers pulling lustily at the rope and charging people twenty-five cents or fifty cents. People went along for novelty as well as the convenience. It was a great lark for the men. They divided the receipts." What was not a lark was the way goods piled up at wharves and freight depots, unable to be transferred. Construction was stalled as bricks could not be delivered. The Great Epizootic was the equivalent today of a giant electric grid failure or an alien attack halting cars, trucks, buses, and subways.

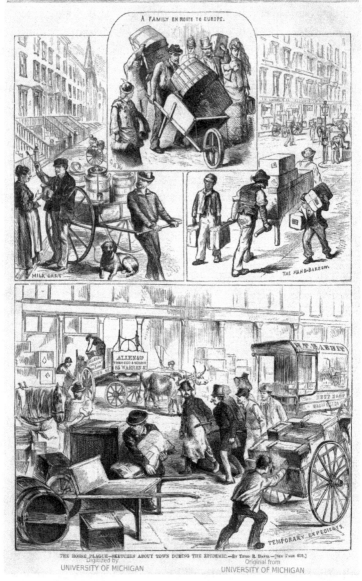

THE HORSE PLAGUE—SKETCHES ABOUT TOWN DURING THE EPIDEMIC.—By THEO. R. DAVIS.—[SEE PAGE 000.]

The Great Epizootic of 1872, which sickened a huge percentage of North America's horses, forced a switch from horsepower to human power. Illustrators for the November 16, 1872, *Harper's Weekly* captured scenes of new transportation modes on city streets.

Baffled veterinarians thought this disease was a distemper or a flu—perhaps diphtheria or blood poisoning. Some called it horse malaria, equine influenza, horse catarrh, horse bronchitis, hippolaryngitis, or other equally fancy and unhelpful names. James Law, a professor of Veterinary Sciences at Cornell University, called it "an epizootic specific fever of a very debilitating type, with inflammation of the respiratory mucous membrane, and less frequently of other organs."

Today it would be clear that the disease spread from horse to horse, likely by infected animals who did not yet exhibit symptoms. This was not obvious to nineteenth-century doctors who favored theories that disease could be spread by airborne miasmas and atmospheric conditions; "germ theory" was still being debated. There did not seem to be concern that the disease could be transmitted to humans. It was thought only horses, mules, and donkeys were affected, although there is evidence that poultry could also contract the illness.

Animal welfare advocates, including the fledgling Massachusetts Society for the Prevention of Cruelty to Animals, sprang into action. Volunteers patrolled the streets to ensure that companies did not force sick horses to work—an act that often proved fatal to the horse. One agent reported that "during the prevalence of the epizootic, I had plenty to do in the preventing the use of horses not fit to work; and my orders were obeyed not, of course, without some grumbling and an occasional 'mild bad word.'" Such actions were recorded in the Boston-based newsletter *Our Dumb Animals* (in this case, "dumb" meant "unable to speak," as illustrated by the tagline, "We speak for those who cannot speak for themselves"), published by George Thorndike Angell, a retired businessman who devoted himself to animal welfare issues. Boston's major animal hospital, Angell Animal Medical Center, is named for him.

The treatment for the sick horses was not that dissimilar to treating a human with a bad flu: bed rest—in this case, stall rest—was crucial. No work for Nellie for at least two weeks. Vets recommended feeding the patients plenty of soft food such as boiled oats and barley, along with treats like carrots and apples, as well as keeping patients' temperatures regulated with blankets. Horse doctors scrambled for answers; they had never seen anything like this disease, and, as it turned out, they never would again.

A humorous portrait of a sick horse from the back pages of the November 16, 1872, *Harper's Weekly*.

Sean Kheraj, an associate professor of Canadian and environmental history in the Department of History at York University in Toronto, Ontario, produced a major study of the horse epizootic, published by Oxford University Press in 2018. Via Zoom, the technology that became ubiquitous due to the Covid-19 pandemic in 2020, I chatted with Kheraj about his research. He is intrigued by urban ecology and networks among cities; in his view, the horse epizootic demonstrated the effect of these networks. He began looking into the epizootic as part of his larger interest in urban livestock—the horses (and cows, pigs, and chickens) that lived in cities well into the nineteenth century. The earliest reports on the outbreak date to a *Toronto Globe* article of October 5, 1872, about a mysterious respiratory disease among the city's horses; this may have originated in farms outside the city, but it quickly spread to Toronto's two thousand horses and then moved on. "The Great Epizootic moved like a fire, burning most fiercely wherever it found ample fuel in the form of horse bodies and a means of reaching those bodies, usually via railroads," Kheraj writes.

He told me the disease was likely a novel mutation of a viral disease to which horses in North America had never been exposed, so it spread easily because there was no acquired immunity. As to *how* it spread, Kheraj analyzed more than 480 newspaper accounts from 1872 and 1873, which showed how the infection largely followed railroad lines, meaning infected horses were being carried from city to city by rail. In October and November, it spread to Boston, New York City, Philadelphia, Baltimore, and Chicago. By early December, it had reached Minneapolis, St. Louis, Kansas City, and New Orleans. By late January, sick horses were reported in Denver and Salt Lake City; by late March, the disease had hit the West Coast. In all, 164 US and Canadian cities and towns were affected. Research indicates the epizootic likely crossed back and forth over the border between Canada and the US five times. It reached Mexico and Cuba, but not Haiti or Jamaica. Europe escaped unscathed.

"All of a sudden everything stops. There's nothing but pedestrian power," Kheraj explained. The epizootic traveled like a wildfire, burning through the horse population and quickly passing. The disease was generally not fatal; from 2 to 5 percent of the stricken horses died. Adoniram B. Judson, a New York–based researcher, calculated that 3.7 percent of the horses in New York City died from the epizootic. With rest, most horses recovered in eight to ten days, although some required three weeks and some exhibited signs of nasal problems even after a month.

The epizootic produced an outpouring of concern for horses and, as Kheraj remarked in his article, some bad poetry. One poem by "R.C.C.," printed in the *Boston Advertiser* was picked up by the November 23, 1873, Hillsboro, Ohio, *Highland Weekly News* as the disease was making its way across North America:

> Gayly the cavalier mounts in the morning
> Dashes the spurs in the sleek glossy side
> Pedestrian pitying, railroad car scorning
> Swift on his thoroughbred charger he'll ride,
> Ah mettlesome rider, brave charger beware
> Each breeze bears distemper. There's death in the air.

...

Ah, whence comes it? Why is it? Wherefore, and what is it?
Smitting the lowly, nor sparing the high;
Worse than the Rinderpest, or the sheep rot is it
Never to cease until the horses all die;
What shall we do for it? What is the best?
Cider, warm blankets, or plenty of rest?

...

Nobly he toiled on the road to East Boston,
Or whirled the swift car over the Roxbury line,
strike now the car bell, its notes will be lost on
The ears that are chilled and give back no sign
Disease has now marked him; his powers are fled;
care for him kindly—he yet is not dead.
Fix the bran mash! If you ever would use him,
Stir as never you stirred it before
We learn to esteem him in fearing to lose him -
Bring the hot water and steam him some more!
There! He is better now;—sponge off that lip —
Harness him up again. Get down the whip.

The animal welfare advocates of *Our Dumb Animals* insisted the disease would convince the public of society's reliance on equine power and lead to better treatment. "If men have bought extra blankets of late, we hope they will not forget to use them in the time to come," one wrote in the November newsletter.

Something more potent than a disease would shine a light on the mistreatment of horses. In 1877, Anna Sewell published *Black Beauty: His Grooms and Companions, the Autobiography of a Horse*. Sewell wrote the book to draw attention to the harsh lives of horses and her narrative told from the viewpoint of a horse was an immediate hit. It has remained in print ever since. In 2012, Pulitzer Prize–winning novelist Jane Smiley told an interviewer on NPR, "*Black Beauty* helped people see animals in a new way. As soon as you say that an animal has a point of view, then it's very difficult to just go and be cruel to that animal. . . . [It showed] readers that the world is full of beings who should not be treated like objects."

It's not hard to see comparisons between the Great Epizootic of 1872 and the human Covid-19 pandemic that emerged in late 2019, even though the victims and the lethality are hugely different. Both diseases had mysterious origins, were first misunderstood, and in many cases minimized. "It was astonishing how many cities would have a headline saying something to the effect of 'We're fine, there's a couple of horses sick, it is really not a big deal and people are really blowing this out of proportion,'" Kheraj told me. "The very next day, two hundred stables have reported sick horses and the streetcar system has shut down."

The Great Epizootic is forever linked to the Great Fire, although the exact effect is difficult to tease out. Boston District Fire Chief John P. Vahey labeled his influential 1972 monograph on the fire "The Epizootic Fire," because, as he said in the introduction, it was one of the many unfortunate conditions that helped spread the fire.

Chief John Damrell was among those horrified by the suffering of the city's horses. "Language fails to express the dreadful features and effect of this unparalleled affliction. Business in all the commercial centers of this great country was at a stand-still. The depots were filled with freight, with no possibility of its speedy removal," he recalled in a speech decades later. "It was no uncommon sight to see men harnessed to horse-cars, to express wagons and even to the city carts used for the collection of garbage; and our sad plight was made the most of by some who seized the opportunity to thoroughly advertise their business by drawing wagons and bands of music around."

Damrell—and other firemen of the day—had special reasons to be alarmed. Two days after the flu began infecting the horses of Boston, thirty-two of the department's thirty-eight horses were down with the disease. Horses were not only essential for the workings of the fire department, but they were also specially trained and, in many cases, were viewed as beloved and respected partners. "Fire horses are the most intelligent and lovable creatures I know of," a veteran driver told a *Boston Post* reporter. Said one author, "The horses are the firemen's pride, their chums in the leisure hours and their partners in danger."

The horses' devotion to their duty is the stuff of legend. An animal welfare newspaper, among its stories of the epizootic, described how two

908   HARPER'S WEEKLY.   [November 23, 1872.

RUINED, AND WINTER AT THE DOOR—AN EPISODE OF THE HORSE PLAGUE.—[Drawn by Paul Frenzeny.]

The "horse plague" prompted animal welfare advocates to draw attention to the equine working conditions and the disease underscored how dependent nine-teenth century society was on these patient, noble beasts. An emotional illustration in the November 23, 1872, *Harper's Weekly* captures this sentiment.

"splendid grays" belonging to a fire company, were attacked by the disease. "One died immediately [and] in spite of all the care and nursing that the firemen lavished on their pet, it was evident the other would soon follow. He sank lower and lower, and it seems as if he had almost drawn his last breath when the fire alarm sounded. The gallant creature started, opened his eyes, made a desperate effort to rise to his feet and take his wonted place before the engine and fell back dead."

Replacing such partners, trained to respond to alarms and stay calm even when cinders and sparks were flying around them, wouldn't be easy even if fire officials could find some to buy—and apparently, they could not. Fire officials reported that they had visited every sales stable in the city, and were unable, either by purchase or hire, to secure any sound horses. They also feared that any new horses might also become infected. "To bring a healthy horse in contact with a sick one will only result in both being unfit," Vahey noted.

On Saturday, October 26, Damrell met with his fourteen assistant engineers and other fire officials to devise a plan for dealing with the shortage of horses. All were aware that any delays in getting to a fire could put the entire city at risk. It was decided that all the apparatus—steam engines, ladder trucks, and hose reels—would be pulled by men. Increased manpower was especially needed for the heavier steam engines, which weighed up to ten-thousand pounds. The group decided to add five hundred men to the department; these substitutes were to be paid a dollar for each alarm they responded to and were to receive twenty-five cents for each hour of fire duty. Ropes were purchased to allow these extra men to drag the apparatus; the Board of Engineers, at 10:00 that night, put the ropes upon their backs and distributed them through the different engine-houses in the entire city.

The switch from horse to manpower could add one or two minutes to the usual eight to ten minutes of time for responding to a first alarm. To make up for this delay, police officers would be allowed to immediately call in a second alarm if a fire were seen above the third floor; normally, they would have to wait for the arrival and approval of an assistant engineer to send a second alarm.

There also was concern that areas of the city might be left uncovered by multiple engines responding to the same fire. In a somewhat complicated set of instructions, the board decided to reduce the number of fire companies that would respond to a first alarm to ensure that other areas of the city were not left without fire coverage. These regulations would even apply to areas of the city that were considered at high risk, including the downtown area, the spot that most concerned Damrell. In general, every available engine in Boston Proper—Companies 3, 4, 6, 7, 8, and 10—would respond to the first alarm for what was known as a "bad box"—that is, an alarm in a congested area of the business district where buildings were high and water pressure low. However, under the emergency regulations only the nearest designated company would respond to a fire alarm, even to a bad box. Damrell ordered that in the case of a third alarm, firemen should seize any horses they could lay their hands on, promising he "would shield them from all responsibility, and if the City Council refused to pay bills caused by such action on their part, [Damrell] would liquidate them from [his] finances." As it turned out, the October 26 contingency plans "turned out to be a serious blunder, none the less deplorable because [they were] the work of brave and conscientious men," as Harold Murdock noted.

From October 26 to November 8, however, this arrangement seemed to be working. The city avoided any serious fires, and, to everyone's great relief, the horses began to recover. As it turned out, the epizootic's effect on the economy was minimal. For example, Kheraj found no records of a street railway company going bankrupt because of horse fatalities.

Nor does the strange disease reemerge. Kheraj told me it's unclear whether the virus—and it's likely it was a virus, although those were as yet undiscovered in the nineteenth century—died out or that horses built up some kind of immunity. What's more likely is that the urban horse population went into decline into the early decades of the twentieth century as gasoline-powered transportation took over. "There aren't thousands of horses in cities anymore. The fuel for spreading an epizootic of this nature just wasn't there," Kheraj said. Ultimately, the Great Epizootic remains one of the most widespread panzootics in modern equine history and still something of a mystery.

I asked Kheraj if the epizootic affected fire departments elsewhere in the way it affected Boston. He had not heard of any such cases. That the Great Fire and the Great Epizootic are tied together seems to be, in his view, "an unfortunate coincidence."

CHAPTER 5

The Spark

No human eye was there to note the little spark, the diminutive flame, and that tiny stream of smoke, that could so easily have been smothered with the foot or extinguished with a cup of water.
—RUSSELL CONWELL, THE GREAT BOSTON FIRE

NOVEMBER 9, 1872, HAS BEEN RAPTUROUSLY DESCRIBED BY CONTEMPO- rary chroniclers as a lovely autumn day in Boston, with mild temperatures, a light breeze, clear and exhilarating air, a cloudless sky, a rosy sunset, and a brilliant full moon. Was the day that the Great Fire began as stunningly beautiful as those writers would have us believe? Or like any Hollywood screenwriter, did they wish to paint a calm portrait of Pleasantville, USA, before the monsters began to roll in?

The truth is that even if that Saturday were a pleasant autumn eve- ning, Boston was not exactly resting easy. Many of the city's horses remained sick, if recovering, and travel was still severely curtailed. While the contingency plans for the fire department's horse shortage seemed to be working, Chief Engineer John Damrell remained on alert, although he was reasonably sure he had done all he could. In the house of Engine Company 7, the T. C. Amory Foreman Daniel Marden and Engineman Charles Riley were on duty. "Looks like it will be a dull night," Marden remarked to Riley, who was cutting off a plug of chewing tobacco. Riley likely happily agreed. East Street was a one-block street on the southern side of the business district, just spitting distance from the wharves of Boston Harbor. Perhaps the men could even smell the ocean in the mild autumn air.

The city went about its Saturday night business. Many recall a singular calm on the streets. In the early evening, shopkeepers and factory owners were shutting down for the weekend. Building maintenance men checked boilers and banked them for the night. Bostonians prepared to go to the theater, some to see *David Garrick,* the comic play about the famed actor. The romantic tale so enthralled one teenager theatergoer that she described the entire plot in her diary. Other citizens were making calls on friends or dining with family or perhaps reading the afternoon papers by illumination of gas lights. Policemen walked their beats. Just after 7:00 p.m. Charlestown police officers, on duty at the Prison Point drawbridge, spotted a glow in the sky. "Must be a fire in Boston," one casually remarked. Workers packed the city's saloons and gin mills, thirsty after a long week. The elite sipped fine liquor in their clubs.

Workers and clubmen weren't the only ones drinking. The Boston Press Association's annual meeting was being held this night. Among the guests were two young reporters delighted at the chance to mix with the grand old men (and, yes, they were all men) of the city's half-dozen daily newspapers. They would rub shoulders with the grizzled reporters and editors of the *Boston Journal,* the *Transcript,* the *Post,* the *Herald,* the *Boston Advertiser,* and the upstart *Boston Globe,* which had just launched in March of that year. Twenty-two-year-old Sylvester Baxter, an *Advertiser* reporter, and his fellow scribe Stephen O'Meara, barely eighteen, were thrilled at being invited to the event, Baxter for the second time and O'Meara for the first. O'Meara later said that the handsomely engraved invitation "gave him a delight even keener than the reception of an honorary university degree."

The ink-stained class gathered at the Revere House, a hotel on Bowdoin Street, just north of Beacon Hill and almost under the shadow of the gold-topped State House, Oliver Wendell Holmes's "Hub of the Solar System." If the menu for the $2 dinner was anything like the feast prepared the previous month for a visiting delegation of Japanese diplomats, the men likely dined on dishes such as roast green goose, boiled shoulder of lamb, and cold turkey with truffles, with sweetbread larded with green peas and soft-shelled crabs as side dishes. Baxter took special note of the three kinds of wine served: sherry, Claret, and Sauterne. Speeches, poems, skits, stories, quips, and puns circled the room. Tom Maguine, a Boston correspondent for *New York Herald*, gave a talk on the skills of interviewing. The men heard the fire bells ring in the distance, but the fire bells were always ringing so they continued their dining.

On hand was Patrick Donahoe, the publisher of Boston's Catholic paper, the *Pilot*, founded as the *Jesuit* in 1829 when Irish immigration to Boston was beginning to pick up. Donahoe had purchased the paper in 1834, changed its name to the *Pilot* and expanded it along with the growing Irish population. He was extremely proud of the fine building housing the newspaper and demanded the removal of a fire hydrant at Franklin and Hawley because—we will speculate—it distracted from the imposing façade or created too much activity in the area. (That act had dismayed Damrell.) Donahoe rose at the conclusion of the dinner to give his annual rendition of "The Star-Spangled Banner"; he was noted for his love of singing even if his voice was not exactly up to the anthem's high notes. A reporter who had stepped out returned, and as Donahoe finished warbling the words, "and the home of the brave," approached the publisher and whispered in his ear. The publisher turned pale and promptly left. Just then, Maguine, who had gone out as well, burst back in. "Gentlemen, are you aware that the whole city is in flames?" he called out.

Every instinct as a reporter triggered, the men rose as one, Baxter and O'Meara among them, and dashed for the door. Outside, a terrible glare lit the streets with a brightness as intense as daylight, the crimson glow veiling the stars. The sullen granite walls of the nearby gothic Bowdoin Square Baptist Church were bathed in gold light. Baxter and O'Meara were about a mile from the corner of Summer and Kingston Streets, where the fire had started, but they could see sheets of flame rising to the left of Beacon Hill. "Our young hearts fairly jumped to our throats," Baxter would recall decades later. The pair sprinted in the direction of the glowing sky. Baxter was about to cover the story of a lifetime and his experiences would shape the green and open spaces in and around Boston in the decades to come.

There are many mysteries about the 1872 fire, but there's little doubt about the ignition point: a six-year-old building at 83-85 Summer Street, at the corner of Kingston. The five-story building, owned by businessman

View down Franklin Street, from Washington St. Destruction of "Pilot" building

Flames consumed the building housing the *Pilot*, the city's Catholic newspaper, as publisher Patrick Donahoe watched. From *Chandler & Co.'s full account of the great fire in Boston and the ruins.*

The fire started in a building at the corner of Summer and Kingston Streets, seen here devastated after the fire. BOSTON PUBLIC LIBRARY

Seman Klous, housed the wholesale dry goods company Tebbetts, Baldwin & Davis, which took up the basement and first floors. Damon Temple & Co., vendors of neckties and hosiery, rented the second and third floors. On the upper floors, Alexander K. Young & Co. manufactured and sold hoop skirts, bustles, and corsets; the company employed about 230 workers. A small steam engine in the rear of the basement provided heat and power to run an elevator, which ran from the basement to the top floor. Built about 1866, it was topped by a Mansard roof and cornices made from wood because, as the architect John R. Hall would later explain, using wood saved construction costs. By 7:00 p.m., all the business owners had left for the day. The building maintenance man William Blaney, generally described as a responsible, hard-working man, had done his work for the evening, checking the furnace and gas before departing. All would later say everything was in perfect order when they left the building.

Alas for doggerel writers, there was no bovine perpetrator to blame for what happened next. That, however, did not prevent the initial chroniclers of the fire to indulge in flowery speculation. Did the boiler man who raked the coals inadvertently let a spark come in contact with combustible material? Did he leave a hot poker among nearby kindling? "Great events hang on little things," portentously declared the writer known as "Carleton," who published a short book on the fire almost immediately after the ashes cooled. "A spark, one little atom of fire, that may be pinched out between the thumb and finger has kindled other sparks." Fire chronicler Russell Conwell was also enthralled with this concept. "No human eye was there to note the little spark, the diminutive flame, and that tiny stream of smoke, that could so easily have been smothered with the foot or extinguished with a cup of water," he wrote in his longer, but no less treacly book on the fire. Subsequent investigation showed that likely something in the basement caught fire and heat rose up the wooden elevator shaft to the ceiling under the handsome, but flammable, Mansard roof. No one will know for sure what caused that initial spark. What happened next is a matter of record.

A little after 7:00 p.m., Major Augustine Sanderson, an Army veteran and a clerk at Boston's Custom House, was attempting to pick up boots he had left for repair at a shop on Bromfield Street. The boots were not ready and, disappointed, Sanderson left the shop and walked on Washington Street toward Winter Street. He stopped to chat with an acquaintance, John S. Holmes, a lawyer. The men almost immediately saw smoke rising about four blocks away on Summer Street. "There must be a fire," Holmes cried. The two ran down Summer Street and, as they neared Kingston Street, started shouting, "Fire, fire!" Sanderson was astonished that no one else was "hallooing fire," since a half-dozen people seemed to be watching the blaze. Through the building's windows, Holmes could see a globe of fire in the basement. Flames were bursting out of the building's elegant Mansard roof. To Sanderson they seemed to burn with a fierce glee.

"You," Sanderson cried to a young lad among those watching the fire. "Why hasn't the fire alarm been pulled?"

"I don't know," replied the boy, excited by the flames crackling nearby.

Sanderson accosted a police officer walking by. "Sir, have you pulled the alarm?"

"Why, yes," the officer said, but added that although he had opened the box and cranked the alarm, nothing happened.

As Sanderson and Holmes watched, the fire appeared to be spreading across a passageway to the roof of another building at its rear on Kingston Street. Holmes was mesmerized by the shocking speed of the blaze; the flame traveled bizarrely fast, almost at right angles, as if by direction, human or divine.

Meanwhile, police officer John M. Page of Station Number Four was walking his nightly beat. He was strolling on Lincoln Street, heading toward Summer Street, when he heard shouts of "Fire." Peering down Summer, he saw flames staining the night sky with streaks of red and orange. Although a building blocked his full view of the fire below, he knew immediately this was a serious burn. He was near Alarm Box 52, at the intersection of Summer, Lincoln, and Bedford Streets. He quickly opened the box with his key, cranked the handle inside, and heard a welcoming ticking sound indicating that the alarm had been sent. As the shouts continued, he cranked the fire alarm again once he was certain the first alarm had gone through. With admirable discipline, Page remained at the box, awaiting new orders.

About a mile away on School Street, Charles Stearns, the officer on duty at the fire alarm headquarters atop Boston City Hall, was reading a newspaper when he noticed a glow in the dark city streets. He was preparing to trigger the striking of the city's bells when the signal from Box 52 came in. He triggered the bells. Five tolls. Pause. Two tolls. That was to indicate Box 52. The time: 7:24 p.m. He waited, watching the glow grow brighter, and another signal arrived. He triggered the second alarm to call in additional men at 7:29 p.m. By that time, however, the fire had been burning for forty-five minutes to an hour.

At the Engine 7 firehouse, Foreman Marden's optimistic forecast for the evening vanished like smoke as someone rang the doorbell, yelling, "Fire on Bedford Street." Before they actually heard the alarm, Marden, Riley, and other men on call, plus volunteers from the street, grabbed the draglines of the T.C. Amory and dragged the 8,970-pound Amoskeag steam engine and hose reel the four or five blocks to the burning Tebbetts, Baldwin & Davis building, arriving in about two minutes. Marden could see right away that his men faced a dangerous fire. The hose was quickly attached to a hydrant on Bedford Street and then plugged into the steamer, its coal-fired engine already churning. The men pointed a stream of water toward the Tebbetts building, but quickly shifted their attention to a nearby building that was smoking. Marden could see that the Summer Street building was gone, and he wanted to focus on limiting the spread. He could also see the streams from Engine 7, while strong, did not reach the top of the building. They continued to "play" the fire, however.

About a minute after Engine 7 arrived, Hose Company 2, the Union, appeared, its 3,080-pound Hunneman hose reel pulled by men from its station at 85 Hudson Street, over a quarter of a mile away. Foreman Nathan S. Brown plugged the hose into a hydrant at Bedford and Kingston Streets. Grabbing the nozzle or "pipe" of the hose, he dragged it toward the Summer Street building, planning to send a stream of water into the cellar. But the fire scene was already getting out of control. Burning debris flew through the air; one piece struck a fireman and knocked off his hat. Brown had to pull the pipe out the window, then turn around and wet the hose behind him to keep it from catching fire from the flying sparks. A twelve-year veteran of the fire department, Brown had never seen a fire move so quickly; it seemed to run like lightning from window to window.

Joseph W. Kinsley, secretary of the Faneuil Hall Insurance Company and a volunteer fireman, happened to be in the Engine 4 firehouse, then located in temporary quarters on Brattle Street, when he heard the fire bell ring. As the gong was striking, Engineer Dexter Dearing threw open the firehouse doors and prepared the hose reel. The company took off as Kinsley cried, "Bedford and Lincoln!" the location of Box 52. The dozen men were joined by others rushing from the City Hotel and Quincy House. Nearing the fire, Kinsley saw the glow in the sky. He turned around and ran back to alert those still at the firehouse to bring their steamer, but the 8,500-pound Amoskeag was already on its way out as Kinsley returned. It arrived at the fire about 7:30 p.m. Technically, Engine 4 had violated the rule, established for the horse flu, that held only one engine company would respond at the first alarm. With the help of about thirty volunteers from the street, the Barnicoat steam engine, its engines already alight, arrived at the fire scene about 7:30 p.m. and plugged into a hydrant near Kingston and Summer Streets.

Now streams were hitting the Tebbetts building from several sides, but it made no difference. Banker Clarence A. Dorr, who was among the crowd watching the fire, said that one of the first things he noted, and what made him think it would be an especially bad fire, was how the water seemed to make no impression on the flames; it just turned into steam. Frederick U. Tracy, the city treasurer who also happened by, marveled at how when firemen would strike a flame with water, the flame would go out and then light up again. Bits of burning clothes, particularly flaming hoop skirts, were driven upward by the heat. The very bones of the building were coming apart.

Granite, seemingly of stern stuff, contains pockets of moisture. When superheated, the water seeks escape and can cause the granite to explode. Hot chunks of granite were sailing skyward, joining the burning debris that was raining down on the firemen. The fire in 83-85 Summer was spreading to nearby buildings on Kingston and Summer Streets at a ferocious speed.

Chief Engineer John Damrell was in his home at 60 Temple Street on Beacon Hill when he heard the fire bells ring. Five bells. Pause, two. Fifty-two. He knew the location; it was considered a "bad box" right in the area about which Damrell had the most concern. Grabbing his helmet, he raced across the Boston Common toward the corner of Bedford, Lincoln, and Summer Streets. When he came to Winter Street, he could see his nightmare coming true. The Tebbetts building was blazing from the basement to the roof, as if it were one vast furnace. In his decades of firefighting, Damrell had never seen anything like this.

To his great relief, he saw that his companies were already at work. Damrell called over one of his men and told him to strike the third alarm. The man found Officer Page, still at Box 52, and Page cranked the third alarm. At the alarm headquarters, Charles A. Stearns noted the time, 7:34 p.m., and set the fire bells ringing. Stearns also struck a fourth alarm,

BOSTON—"INTO THE JAWS OF DEATH."

In one of the most dramatic illustrations of the fire from the November 30 front page of *Harper's Weekly* six firemen look "into the jaws of death," as the caption says.

on his own volition, at 7:45, to call in all fire companies. He even triggered a fifth alarm, even though the fourth alarm would call out all available units.

Damrell saw Foreman Brown in an alleyway behind the Tebbetts building and ordered him to take his line into an adjoining building, which was catching fire. Brown ran with the hose to the building's third floor to play water on the windowsills and frames that were dancing with flames. He and his men stayed until their water was cut off; another engine had plugged into their hydrant and the pressure dropped. "Get out of the building," came the command. Brown and his company complied. Within ten minutes the walls of the Tebbetts building collapsed, followed by those in the one Brown and his men had just vacated.

Summer Street was now so hot that firefighters had to lay in the gutters, directing their water streams from behind makeshift fire shields and barriers of wet crates. Coming upon the scene was Thomas Leighton Jenks, a member of the Board of Aldermen, who called out to Damrell, with a kind of nervous irony, "Captain, you have got a fearful fire."

Damrell replied bluntly, "Yes, and the city is doomed. This fire will go to the water, for I have not sufficient force at my command to stay its progress."

"Do you mean what you say?" Jenks said, caught off guard.

"I do and know whereof I speak." Damrell responded.

Damrell told Jenks to go to the Union Telegraph Office and request help from every city and town within fifty miles of Boston.

"Is this a request, or shall I execute this as an order, from you as chief?"

"An order, and without delay," replied Damrell.

Jenks would do as asked, but the calls for help were hampered as the telegraph offices were closed for the evening. Yet slowly the word got out that Boston was facing destruction and firefighters from around the region prepared to head to the Hub.

Damrell was seeing the Chicago fire unfold in front of him. From the speed and ferocity of what was fast becoming a firestorm—unlike anything he had ever seen—he knew the city's fate depended on responding with everything that could be mustered and would require every bit of his firefighting knowledge. He did not yet know that his every action, and every twist and turn of the next twenty-two hours would be scrutinized, critiqued, and fiercely debated.

CHAPTER 6

Out of Control

The first principle, in fighting a fire, is to make as direct and as close an application of the water as possible. It has been a great study with the members of the Board of Engineers how to direct our water upon the burning mass itself in the building and not to waste one drop of water.
—JOHN S. DAMRELL, 1872

IN THE GROVE HALL NEIGHBORHOOD OF DORCHESTER, ABOUT FOUR miles from downtown Boston, Seman Klous was preparing for bed when someone pounded on his door and shouted, "Mr. Klous, come to the city quickly. Boston is on fire and your property is involved."

Looking out the window, Klous saw a great cloud of smoke and a red glow in the sky. He quickly harnessed a horse and galloped toward the city. An immigrant from Germany who ran a successful fur hats and caps business, Klous had only six years earlier built an imposing building at 83-85 Summer Street. He now drove his horse in its direction. When he arrived, sweating, his horse panting, all he could do was watch his building burn, along with everything in it.

The word "conflagration" is bandied about by tabloid headline writers, but to firefighters, it represents a fire that burns so hot it can ignite structures across streets and other barriers. Damrell saw that he had a conflagration when fire jumped Summer Street from the Tebbetts building and ignited a Mansard roof in a building on Otis Street, which was occupied by wholesale dealers in dry and fancy goods. To his relief, additional fire companies were arriving at the fire scene, the men straining at the shafts where the horses—which had been stricken by the mysterious

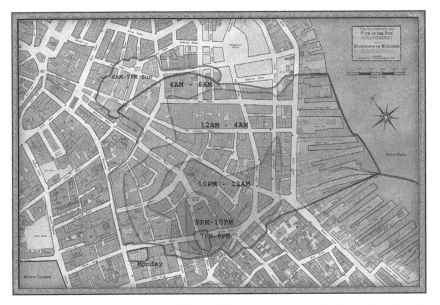

This map showing the progress of the 1872 fire was created by Bruce Twickler of Docema for his documentary on the Great Boston Fire. Twickler based the map on testimony after the fire to ensure a more accurate depiction of how the fire spread.

illness—were usually positioned. Ladder Company Number One arrived at 7:31 p.m., and Hose Company Number One and Hose Company Number Eight came a minute later. By 8:00 p.m., twenty-six companies, nearly all pulled by men, had responded. Their usual response time was increased by five to ten minutes.

A bystander, Joseph W. Kinsley, saw that the fire had jumped Otis Street and set out to alert Cambridge firemen. He managed to find someone who would run to East Cambridge; the first company from Cambridge arrived at the fire scene about 8:12 p.m. Fire was creeping steadily up both sides of Summer Street, crawling from roof to roof as though, one observer said, there was a rivalry between the two sides as to which would outstrip the other in speed.

Damrell barked orders: Bring all extra hose to City Hall. Send a messenger to the alarm superintendent to send a special train to Worcester and bring all the firemen and apparatus possible from towns along the line. The engine man of Company Four called out that they could no longer remain in their position—they were being blasted by the heat and assailed by blocks of exploding granite and burning debris. Damrell told him to put on another piece of suction and swing his engine farther around on the corner; he had to remain there until he burned the instruments off his engine. He would have hose-men play streams on the engine and his firemen alternately, so that they could hold their position. The engine man promised to stay until he was ordered to leave.

Damrell attempted to position the arriving companies in a formation that could hold back the flames around the Tebbetts building. That was proving impossible. Rather than presenting a solid wall of flame, the fire continued leaping from building to building, catching here and there on the roofs and burning the timbers in the comparatively thin brick walls.

Engine Company 9 from East Boston took up a position in Church Green, near Box 52. Engine 10 tried to hold the corner at Summer and Arch Streets, while Ladder 1 was at Summer and Otis Streets. They had to fall back when the heat grew too great and the streams of water faltered, which was happening with alarming frequency. Because hydrants were spaced so far apart, it was difficult to amass fire engines together, and the buildings were built so close together that they could only be approached from one side. Damrell didn't yet have his requested fire boat—it was still under construction—so he called for positioning the tugboat *Louis Osborn* at the wharf at the foot of Summer Street with hoses brought on board.

"For God's sake, hold this corner at all hazard," Damrell yelled to Assistant Engineer William Green, who was taking a stand at the intersection of Devonshire and Summer Streets. "I will, if you can give me the water," Green grimly replied. Damrell would have been most happy to do so but didn't have the water to give: the streams were weakening. He did, however, order all the streams on that line shut off, allowing Green to get a stronger stream that he aimed toward the roofs.

But as Damrell had warned, even the strongest streams could not reach the tops of the new buildings, where the fire was spreading roof to roof. To the south of the original fire site, firemen were able to hold the fire within a couple of blocks of Summer Street. Flames relentlessly crept

THE FIRE COMING INTO DEVONSHIRE STREET FROM WINTHROP SQUARE

The fire spread along Devonshire Street, triggering a mad rush by merchants and residents to cart away merchandise and belongings. Others came just to gawk at the flames. Illustration from *Frank Leslie's Weekly*, November 23, 1872.

north, east, and west. The heat was so intense that the stone coping of a building sixty feet from the fire burst and crumbled. One piece fell and severed the hose of Engine 4, forcing the men to pull back to patch the hose.

Strangely, the fire seemed to move against the wind. The winds that night were mild, varying from northwest to north at five to nine miles per hour. But as the fire grew hotter, it created its own winds of thirty to thirty-five miles per hour. On contact with this growing firestorm, streams of water turned to steam, dissipating before even touching the flames. "The magnificent structures which were rapidly burned one after the other seemed to shine with a heat almost white in its intensity, before succumbing to the devouring element. The largest stone warehouses in the city would take fire in their Mansard roofs and in less than half an hour would be one sheet of livid flames from roof to basement. Can any one fact more vividly describe the rapidity with which the flames spread than this?" a *Boston Transcript* reporter wrote.

Between 8:00 and 10:00 p.m., the fire moved steadily northwest toward Winthrop Square. Walls of burning buildings began to collapse with thunderous crashes that sent debris flying skyward. Gas from the main lines continued to pour out, pooling and igniting. Out-of-town fire companies were pouring in from Charlestown, Chelsea, Somerville, Mattapan, and Medford, their equipment hauled by hand. Some companies were unable to connect their hoses to the older Boston hydrants; they were directed to the cisterns where they could draw water directly or were further delayed as they hunted for couplings that could let them hook up to hydrants.

Alerted by telegram, the region was learning that Boston was on fire. Companies from Salem, Massachusetts; Providence, Rhode Island; Biddeford, Maine; and Portsmouth, New Hampshire, loaded their engines on rail cars and left for Boston.

At about 10:00 p.m., reporters Baxter and O'Meara arrived at Summer Street, now arched with flames. They circled the perimeter of the fire three times; to the south it had not crossed Essex Street, but when the men ran up Arch Street, they saw buildings ablaze in Winthrop Square. They watched the edifice called the Beebe Block, what Baxter called the handsomest mercantile building in Boston, burn in a magnificent spectacle. The whole interior was a roaring furnace, contrasting with the white heat that lit the window openings. The granite walls seemed almost black, yet architectural details showed plainly in the light that reflected from all around. A building on Devonshire, just across the street from the Beebe Block went up in an instant—one moment untouched, the next all ablaze. Heat seared Baxter's face as Mansard roofs ignited like paper under a match and granite seemed to turn to sand when hit by water from fire hoses. The reporters rushed up Franklin Street, its west side burning, to Federal Street. They watched as the fire crossed Purchase Street and reached the wharves that lined the harbor.

Damrell was beset by problems on all sides. Purchase Street was lined with tenement houses and although some of them were burning, occupants were focused on rescuing their possessions rather than fleeing for their lives. As he tried to supervise an evacuation, a little lad about twelve years old came up and took the chief by the hand, begging him to save his father and mother. "Can you point to where they are?" Damrell asked.

Breaking out of flames in Beebe Block. Saturday Night, Nov. 9.

The Beebee Block was viewed as one of the finest buildings in the commercial district. It burned to the ground during the fire. From Chandler & Co.'s full account of the great fire in Boston and the ruins, published just a few days after the fire.

The boy pointed to a building engulfed with flames. Damrell rushed inside, but he could not get above the first floor because of the smoke and flames. Coughing, he rushed out, picked up the boy, and carried him to some onlookers, asking them to keep him safe. Meanwhile, residents were tumbling goods down from windows and blocking staircases. Damrell ordered firemen to open windows and evacuate people as quickly as possible. He never learned what happened to the little boy or his parents.

Damrell called for a police officer, telling him, "Go to the Deputy Chief of Police at City Hall and tell him that I want fifty policemen to go into any gentleman's house or carpet store, wherever goods of that kind might be found, and press into service any men and to cover the roofs and windows of every building that it was possible to cover, with carpets. Tell them they have authority from the Chief Engineer." Damrell knew this was an effective firefighting technique, but for some reason his

FRANKLIN STREET IN FLAMES.

Damrell hoped to make a stand at Franklin Street, but its buildings became fodder for the Fire Fiend, as shown in this illustration from Coffin's *The Story of the Great Fire.*

WINTHROP SQUARE IN FLAMES.

Winthrop Square in flames, from Charles "Carleton" Coffin's *The Story of the Great Fire.*

instructions weren't carried out—except in one exceptional case, high-lighted in Chapter 8.

A tenet of firefighting is to set a plan for action and a back-up plan in case the first plan fails. Damrell needed to get a fix on where the fire was spreading. He ran to Milk Street, where he smashed in the door of the tallest building he could see and climbed to the sixth-floor roof. He could now view every corner of the fire. Where could he make a more success-ful attack? Could he deploy gunpowder to blow up buildings and create a fire break? With nothing to burn, the fire might be halted. He focused on Franklin Street northwest of Winthrop Square. It was one of the widest streets in the district and the heart of the wool trade that had become so important to the city. If he could mass his engines there, he might be able to hold back the fire.

He returned to the fire scene with renewed energy and met a com-pany arriving from Charlestown, ordering them into position on Franklin

Street. "This is the key of the fire," he told the foreman. "If you keep it here
. . . I have sufficient force to stop it the other way if I can get the water."

By now, Winthrop Square was a total loss. Iron shutters had warped
and melted. Granite columns crumbled and fell, while great piles of cot-
ton and woolen fabrics had provided fuel for the fire. Shouting commands,
Damrell massed the Boston and Charlestown departments on Franklin
Street. And then the water gave out; the streams dropped to nothing.
Firemen had to pull back. Whether firefighters could have stopped the
fire there, Damrell could not say positively, but he and his men were dis-
heartened to near despair. "Even Franklin Street, with its high walls of
stone, cemented like a fortress . . . bowed before the fire king," Russell
Conwell wrote in his book on the fire.

CHAPTER 7

The Fire Fiend

All day Sunday the fire burned & last night the sky still glowed red with the tons of coal smoldering on the wharves & small fires breaking out all over the burnt district. Soldiers guarded the streets, for tottering walls were dangerous, & thieves so thick the police had no place to hold them when caught.

—Louisa May Alcott
From a letter to her sister,
Anna Alcott Pratt, Nov. 10, 1872

To many observers, the fire began to assume a persona: it was the Fire Fiend, a monster intending to devour all it could. "The Fire Fiend was abroad again and most mercilessly did he wield his powers for destruction among that mass of beautiful, costly superb bazaars of trade," Charles Coffin wrote in his contemporary book on the fire, under the pen name "Carleton." Reporters imbued the Fire Fiend with malignant purpose. Said the *Boston Globe*, "Buildings would fall crunching and thundering to the ground in huge masses with the roar and relentless fury of an avalanche. The air was filled with burning cinders that were hurled wildly above, where they hovered confusedly for a moment and then descended like a shower of gold to earth, where they hissed, sputtered and crackled as though in malicious glee." The sounds were overwhelming. "The heavy rumbling thunder that rolled forth as masses of masonry dashed to the ground, the welling groan that incessantly issued from the throats of the agitated multitude, mingling with the sharp class of engine bells and the whistle and hiss of escaping steam, making a din that was fiendish in its

The fire at its height,—looking towards Winthrop Square, from the North, Saturday night.

The fire at its height on Saturday night as illustrated by Chandler & Co. account.

savagery. The heat was almost unbearable to those in its vicinity." Currents and countercurrents of rarified air rushed in every direction with the force of a tornado, rendering human power impotent to resist what was being called a "Niagara of destruction." Among the most-quoted descriptions is this one by Russell Conwell: "Then came the war-dance of the fire-fiends, with all its hideous concomitants—its snapping, rattling, bellowing, crashing; its steams of hellish flame, and puffs of swarthy smoke, as though the earth had yawned and loosed those weird, traditional denizens of its fiery depths . . . It burned as fires have burned before and may burn again; except that never before in its history has it had such solid fortresses to capture, and so much stone and iron to destroy."

Sometime after midnight as the fire continued to rage, reporters Baxter and O'Meara climbed to the top of the Parker House, a Boston institution since 1855, on School Street just across from the City Hall. Here they watched as the *Pilot* building on Franklin Street became a bonfire that shot flames far into the sky. The sky was perfectly clear; the stars shone through a scarlet veil, a different sort of star-spangledness than what Patrick Donahue, in his blissful ignorance, had sung just hours earlier at the Boston Press Association dinner. They stayed on the roof until they saw the sun rise out of the sea above the still-raging flames. By 4:00 a.m., six or seven wharves were ablaze.

As if the fire weren't enough, firemen had to contend with another issue—a huge crush of onlookers and merchants that made it difficult for firemen to move around the city. It was not unusual for fires to attract crowds of people; watching fire was a common form of urban entertainment, but an astonishingly large number of people thronged the streets, mingling with the fire apparatus. Initially the area had a macabre carnival atmosphere, with drunken revelers as well as giddy onlookers. During the Chicago Fire, saloons stayed open and now Bostonians were also managing to find something to drink—one liquor outlet even gave away its hooch as the fire threatened to burn it all. "The city was filled with jittering inebriates," Lucius Beebe, a Boston historian whose father lost his leather business on Pearl Street in the fire, wrote in his 1935 book,

BOSTON—SCENE IN CHAUNCEY STREET—MERCHANTS DEFENDING THEIR GOODS AGAINST THIEVES AND ROUGHS.—[SEE PAGE 931.]

Merchants on Chauncy Street defended their merchandise from thieves; others gave away their goods rather than see them burn. *Harper's Weekly*, November 30, 1872.

Boston and the Boston Legend. He gleefully recounted, "There were souses everywhere. The downtown area was full of drunks. They tripped over hose lines and hurrahed and howled when roofs fell in. Often they fell into manholes and had to be [pulled] out by impatient and overworked policemen."

Not everyone was drinking. Businessmen and bankers pushed their way through the crowds, trying to move merchandise, money, or important papers away from the fire's path. Clerks rushed to their employers' stores and carried away goods; truckmen and teamsters harnessed whatever horses could move and galloped to the scene of devastation, where they charged high prices to remove goods. Some building owners attempted to bribe, browbeat, or otherwise influence firefighters to desert their positions and take up others that might save their buildings. At one point, Damrell had to intervene when a businessman angrily demanded help even though firemen could see that his building was gone.

With their buildings facing sure destruction, some merchants opened their stores and invited people to help themselves to the contents, rather than see it burn. Witnesses said they walked knee-deep in silk, laces, and elegant shawls thrown out from the great stores. However, firefighters saw this not as generosity but as a fearful and demoralizing act, as it encouraged looting. It was impossible to distinguish looters from those carting off what desperate merchants or businessmen had given away. Damrell experienced this himself. "There were whole blocks of stores that were completely filled with the greatest number of thieves I ever saw. I never saw anything like it. I went into one building, and took my fire hat, and beat out fifty to sixty people. The awnings were all burning, and they never touched an awning: so eager were they to plunder, that they never attempted to save property. I am not certain that they did not set fire to get an additional amount of plunder," he later said.

The lucky ones who escaped with their household goods, along with merchants carrying their products, began filling Boston Common. Families huddled together, surrounded by their possessions, hoping their homes might be spared. Baxter saw one woman carrying a washboard; a girl lugged a bucket of coal. On a heap of furniture lay a boy without an overcoat, fast asleep in the chill air. Other reporters marveled at the

MILITARY FORCING BACK THE CROWD IN LIBERTY STREET.

The military was called in to try to keep order on the streets; here they are shown trying to keep crowds on Liberty Street away from fire-fighting efforts. *Harper's Weekly*, November 30, 1872.

man who hauled a feather bed down the stairs but hurled a mirror from a window. The piteous mixed with the absurd. An older woman pushed her way among the crowd, crying and shrieking for "Clara," and enlisting the sympathy of bystanders who couldn't tell if the sobbing, half-deranged woman was looking for a child. Firemen tried to question her, but she could only moan and wring her hands. Then with a wild shriek of joy, she darted forward, crying, "Clara, Clara!" Crouching in a corner was a large white cat with singed fur, who, with curved back and swollen tail, stood hissing and spitting with fear. As the old lady stooped to pick up her darling, the ungrateful cat clawed her face and ran off, her mistress in frantic pursuit, as the onlookers hooted with laughter and relief.

Both the wealthy and the poor raced to protect their belongings. Charles Eliot, Harvard's relatively new president, worried about the Boston holdings of the Cambridge institution. He and Harvard treasurer Nathaniel Silbee raced to Silbee's office on Washington between Water and State Streets to grab the college's original record books and important papers. Eliot also worried about Harvard's securities in the vaults of the State Street Bank. He and Silbee, joined by Francis B. Crowninshield of the Harvard Corporation, walked the trove of materials back to Cambridge. Eliot carried the bag with Silbee on his right, Crowninshield following, his hand on a pistol in his coat pocket. Within an hour, they reached a bank in Cambridge, where they stashed the documents.

The leaders of other institutions were rescuing assets as well. Paul Adams, president of the Five Cent Savings Bank, walked to the bank's headquarters on School Street, put $11 million in money and securities in a satchel, and carried it to his home at 123 Charles Street. Wearing a top hat and frock coat and wielding a double-barreled gun, he spent the next day and night seated in his front hall, guarding the funds.

Meanwhile, *Pilot* publisher Patrick Donahoe could only watch the destruction of his business headquarters, a six-story granite edifice called the Donahoe Building, at the corner of Franklin and Hawley Streets. It housed the printing plant for the *Pilot*, a bookstore, a travel agency, and a church-goods store, which served as the largest religious-goods emporium in New England.

While many merchants did what they could to save assets, others demanded firefighters do more to help. Benjamin Pickering, foreman of the Salem Hose Company 5, was working on Pearl Street when he was approached by a man who owned a building there. He later described in detail what happened.

"Who are you?" the man demanded.

"I am foreman of Lafayette Hose, of Salem," Pickering responded.

The man said, "If you will take your hose round the building, you can save it."

Pickering turned to his engineer. "What do you say, Capt. Osborne?"

"I think you had better go round," replied the captain.

As Pickering was moving the hose, the owner of a building on the opposite side of the street came over to complain that Pickering was unfair and showing "partiality."

"Why?" Pickering asked.

"You are saving that man's building and letting mine burn," the man replied.

Pickering shook his head. "I can't take care of both, and I think I can save that building."

"You can save my building, if you stay here," the man said.

VIEW OF THE RUINS, FROM PEARL-STREET.

Pearl Street was transformed into a twisted, grotesque landscape by the fire. The *Illustrated London News*, December 7, 1872.

"I don't have anything to do with that," Pickering said. "My duty always is to obey superior orders, and my orders are to go round and save the other building."

The man cursed and swore, but Pickering didn't pay any attention to him. He told his men to take the hose and go round the building as ordered. "I don't think that any one stream could have taken care of any of the buildings that were there, they were so large," Pickering later said.

As the fire raged, reporters roamed the street gathering stories, not always verified. Many were collected in the *History of the Great Conflagration or Boston and Its Destruction*, published quickly after the fire. An unnamed author describes the brave fireman "who crawled into a cellar on Congress Street and let off the steam from three overheated boilers which threatened every instant to explode. It was so hot that his comrades kept two streams of water playing on him while he performed this perilous duty."

The following, while dramatic, may be of doubtful veracity:

There were not a few heart-rending scenes to record, which makes the pen falter. A little girl whose name is unknown, was in one of the upper rooms of a house on Washington Street, looking out of a window at the fire. She was seen from the street to be struck full in the face by a piece of burning wood and knocked back into the room from which in an incredible short space of time the flames burst forth in great masses. In a moment or two the whole building was wrapped in fire.

No prose was too purple for chroniclers of the fire, such as the writer with the pen name of Carleton. "The wind had now increased in violence till it had become a most furious gale, blowing smoke and firebrands into the faces of the crowd, and beating back the firemen who stood as firmly, as possible to their work. The skies were wild with the reflection of the lurid flames which hissed along the streets and ran from house to house, licking and lapping them and writhing about them like fiery serpents," he wrote.

Even as their reporters prowled the fiery streets, the proprietors of the *Boston Transcript*, the *Journal*, *Post*, and *Globe* began to lock up their type and make other necessary preparations for moving what they could. Everything portable was sent down to the lower floors, ready to be carted away in a moment. *Saturday Evening Gazette* editors and reporters worked up to the last possible moment on Sunday morning, escaping from the burning building with just enough time to take only one impression from the type already laid out for the magazine, which was saved for many years.

When the Federal Street printing room of the magazine *American Homes* was threatened, the compositor and his wife scooped up equipment to carry away, the wife balancing a drawer of type on her head. By midnight, it was clear that the magazine's main office on Water Street

EXCITEMENT IN STATE-STREET—REMOVAL OF PAPERS AND VALUABLES.

Desperate businessmen on State Street tried to save company books and records. *The Illustrated London News*, December 7, 1872.

THE BIG FIRE.

The printing rooms of AMERICAN HOMES were on Federal street, Boston; the counting-room was on Water street, a short distance off, and when the big fire swept across that section of Boston, Nov. 9th and 10th, our electrotype plates, new type and complete composing-room and press-room fixtures, hundreds of costly wood-cuts, thousands of chromos, tens of thousands of magazines, and other stock and fixtures too numerous to mention, were devoured by the Fire Fiend with a rapidity and a thoroughness which was peculiarly exasperating, as well as excessively costly. During the progress of the flames one of the compositors and his good wife visited the composing-room, and hastily secured a few forms of type and cuts, the

Water street, and the goods were stored in the counting-room for safe (?) keeping. But the flames pushed onward with an irresistible power, and it was plain soon after midnight that the building on Water street must be consumed. While the authorities were arranging to blow up the building to prevent further spread of the flames, the head-book keeper of AMERICAN HOMES was endeavoring, with the aid of our engineer, engraver, and two or three volunteers, to save what he could of

the stock in the counting-room, and right loyally and nobly did they work in the few moments alloted to them. Before they were obliged to leave the building one end had been blown off, and one of the AMERICAN HOMES horses, who had been brought over for the emergency, scarcely knew whether he was on his head or his heels, the noise and excitement were so intense. The express

lady carrying the latter in a large drawer in the manner indicated in the drawing. At that time, 10.30 P.M., Saturday, the fire had not reached

The staff of *American Homes* waged a desperate effort to save what they could from magazine's printing room and offices. The compositor and his wife scooped up equipment to carry away, the wife balancing a drawer of type on her head; boxes were loaded into a cart pulled by a horse "which scarcely knew whether he was on his head or heels, the noise and excitements were so intense." The magazine later printed a story and illustrations of the harrowing night.

was destined for destruction; the staff tried to save what they could, but one end of the building blew up before they even left. Type, subscription lists, business books, and about twenty-five hundred lithographs were piled into a horse-drawn wagon and the staff took off, the building burning behind them. Most of the remaining stock, including plates, type, woodcuts, and tens of thousands of magazines were "devoured by the Fire Fiend, with a rapidity and thoroughness that was peculiarly exasperating as well as excessively costly," according to the magazine's editors. When the fire came within two blocks of the Western Union Telegraph Office, operators grabbed their instruments and prepared to vacate. By midnight, the flames burned across High Street, Purchase Street, and Broad Street, reaching the wharves along the harbor.

Fire always attracts the curious and the voyeuristic, but perhaps no fire in history was viewed by so many of America's literati of the likes of Oliver Wendell Holmes, William Lloyd Garrison, Alexander Graham Bell, and Louisa May Alcott.

Large urban fires seemed to hold a particular fascination for Garrison, the famed abolitionist. At 2:00 in the morning on March 29, 1868, he awakened his son Frank to witness the burning of a church in the neighborhood. He spent much of the night of November 9, 1872, observing first-hand the flames that leveled stores, business blocks, and warehouses in central Boston; he must have noticed the destruction of Merchants Hall, the first location of his magazine, the *Liberator*. "It is tempting to speculate on the association Garrison might have been making between the human destruction of slavery and the devastation of fire in a crowded city," one of his biographers wrote. Or perhaps Garrison, like many fire buffs of today, was simply mesmerized by the spectacle of his city burning. "It was a sad, wonderful and fascinating sight to see the ruins from Washington Street, extending from Summer to Milk Streets and thence sweeping broadly to the water," he wrote in a letter.

Among the many who rushed to help with the fire was a young teacher of the deaf with a flair for invention. Twenty-five-year-old Alexander Graham Bell wrote to his family to say he had "in common with half the male population of Boston [been] out all night on Saturday. Fire broke out again today and is now raging. More money destroyed than at

Chicago. I am dead tired so will turn [in]. I shall write you full details via the *Globe* Newspaper. Look out for the account of an eye-witness signed A.G.B. and buy some copies." He emphasized his tales to come in another letter, "I have had some thrilling experiences. Look out for the Globe." Alas for history, the editors of the *Globe* did not see fit to publish his observations (as far as I could tell), and it's unclear whether Bell kept a copy. His observations on the fire may have been lost, but less than four years later, he received a patent for the telephone.

As Boston's Episcopal Bishop, the Reverend Phillip Brooks, a prominent theologian who is associated with the Christmas carol "O Little Town of Bethlehem," thought the fire would never stop as long as there was something left to burn. "Street after street went like paper. There were sights so splendid and awful as I never dreamed of," he wrote. Brooks was not a disinterested bystander. He and his sexton went to his church, Trinity Church, which stood at the corner of Summer and Washington Streets, to keep an eye on the building. The church lasted through the night but at about 4:00 a.m., the rear of the building caught fire. Seeing that there was no chance of saving the structure, Brooks grabbed some books and robes and fled, his sexton, by habit, opening and fastening back the church doors as if for a service. "She burnt majestically," Brooks wrote. "Her great tower stands now solid as ever, a most picturesque and stately ruin. She died in dignity."

Oliver Wendell Holmes Sr., who would also write a poem about the fire, described watching the fire in a somewhat more jocular tone. "I went out, thinking I would go to Commonwealth Ave. to get a clear view of it. As I went in that direction, I soon found I was approaching a great conflagration. There was no getting very near the fire: but that night and the next morning I saw it dissolving the great high buildings, which seemed to melt away in it." He watched as the fire crept toward his bank and "my deposits, and millions of others with them, and [I] thought how I should like it to have them wiped out with that red flame that was coming along clearing everything before it. But I knew all was doing that could be done . . . and managed to sleep both Saturday and Sunday nights tolerably well."

Phillip Brooks, one of the country's most prominent theologians.

NIGHT SCENE. SUMMER STREET (Billings).

The fire rampaged along Summer Street and torched the venerable Trinity Church. "She burnt majestically," said Rev. Phillip Brooks. R.H. CONWELL, *HISTORY OF THE GREAT FIRE IN BOSTON*

Flush with the success of the publication of *Little Woman* just a few years earlier, Louisa May Alcott was living on Beacon Hill and thoroughly enjoying the financial benefits from her creation. She was churning out short stories and immersing herself in feminist causes such as Women's Right to Labor and Women's Right to Vote. On November 9, she had heard the fire bells—but like so many others, paid no mind until about 9:00 p.m., when young men in the neighborhood rushed by to say that Summer Street was burning and the city was in panic. She described the scene in an evocative letter to her sister, Anna (known to the literary world as the model for oldest sister Meg March in *Little Women*). "So I bundled up and went out to see the fire like a true descendant of Fire Warden May," a reference to an ancestor on her mother's side. She would be up all night watching a "very splendid and terrible sight. . . . The red glare, the strange roar, the flying people, all made the night terrible, and I kept thinking of 'The Last Days of Pompeii,'" she wrote. She went on to describe blazing boards and great pieces of cloth and rolls of paper

Louisa May Alcott called the fire a "Splendid and terrible sight."

flying in all directions, falling on roofs and spreading the fire. Granite blocks of buildings on Franklin Street went down like houses of cards and heavy cornices peeled off as if made of paper. Alcott joined the spectators thronging the streets, only backing away as a load of powder was brought in to blow up a block. From the Granary Cemetery on Beacon Hill, she watched the fire, admittedly enjoying the spectacle, until she went home at about 2:00 a.m. to warm up. She fed tea and cake to the "poor, wet, tired boys" who came bringing their employers' books for safe keeping. She gave an extra piece of cake to one young boy who had been sent to fetch a basket of wine from an office on fire; he had left the wine and instead rescued a mother cat and her kittens.

Even as Alcott and her guests relaxed, a friend who would lose a store to the fire rushed in to announce that the fire was coming their way and they had to ready themselves to leave. Alcott, with the aplomb of a woman who longed for adventure, piled her current manuscript, her one good gown, a pair of new boots, and a few books into a blanket, ready for the signal to flee.

Fortunately, it never came. On Sunday, she ventured out again, even as the fire still burned, and saw a spotted dog, howling over the ruins of a house. Louisa resolved to put him in a story, as he was "so pathetic and so very ugly."

Meanwhile, after losing the fight at Franklin Street, Damrell regrouped his forces, now swelled by engines from the communities of Brookline, Malden, Medford, Newton, and Lawrence. Twelve miles to the north, Wakefield firemen gathered at a local drug store then together dragged their two hand-pumped engines to the fire, arriving about 11:45 a.m. on Sunday. The fire was still out of control.

CHAPTER 8

Guts and Gunpowder

The writer met Chief Damrell on State Street, near the old State House, and the features of his blackened, burned, and haggard face could be read as in a book [about] the great anxiety that was stirring his very soul. "One word, Captain," said the reporter. "What of the prospect?" Shaking his head, and with a gesture that told more than the words: Bad, bad, bad. "God help burning Boston," said he, and on he went through a dense volume of smoke to where a corps of his nearly suffocated and famished men were struggling with the fiend.

—Author Unknown
History of the Great Conflagration of
Boston and Its Destruction, 1872

The firemen fought the Fire Fiend with courage that bordered on madness. They stayed at their posts until driven off by heat. They dodged chunks of flying granite, brushed flaming cinders from their coats, and coughed in the smoke-saturated air. They climbed shaky ladders to the roofs of burning buildings to douse flames from above. They drenched each other with water to keep from incineration. They worked through Saturday night and into Sunday without food or a break. When their steam engines ran short of coal, they whistled for the coal cart, and if that did not come, they broke up whatever wood or flammable material they could find—furniture or boxes—and stoked their engines.

Boston firemen worked alongside those from Brookline, Somerville, Cambridge, Chelsea, Reading, Malden, Wayland, Lynn, Lawrence, and Worcester. By Sunday morning, companies from Connecticut, New

Hampshire, Rhode Island, and Maine were unloading their engines from train cars and pulling them toward the maelstrom of heat and smoke. A total of forty-two steam-engine companies, four hand-pumped engines, fifty-three hose companies, and three ladder trucks, representing about 1,700 men, heeded the call to come to Boston. Observers would say they never saw more bravery or skill than among these men.

About ninety-five miles away in Biddeford, Maine, James E. Gowan, a volunteer fireman, heard the school bells ringing. He rushed to the firehouse and discovered the chief was asking for volunteers to go to Boston. As a young man, Gowan had been bitterly disappointed that the chief would not let him go to a big fire on July 4, 1866, in Portland, because he was "too small for a big fire like that." So, he was determined to get on the special train that would take the Biddeford and Saco, Maine, firemen and a hose reel to Boston. This time, he succeeded. The companies arrived about 11:00 a.m. on Sunday and were quickly directed to Washington Street, where they played streams on the Jordan Marsh department store for hours. The ears, feet, and hands of the firemen were frostbitten. Gowan stayed in Boston until the next afternoon. "I never suffered so much with the cold in my life as I did that day," he recalled forty years later.

Assistant Boston Engineer John S. Jacobs took a man by the collar and pulled him out of a basement, carried him to the next building, and threw him up onto the roof. The man "was there like a bull-dog and would not leave until he was driven out," he recalled later. Jacobs had to tell his men more than once to come out of a building because he could see fire dangerously moving up a stairway or creeping underneath the eaves. Jacobs himself was nearly blinded by the smoke and heat; he had to work on holding his eyes open. He felt no need of food.

Right beside the firemen was their chief. Stories would circulate that night of Damrell's fearlessness and steady manner, and also of his curtness and even rudeness. One report—picked up in newsprint—said he had gone mad and was taken to a hospital for the insane. Others reported he was calm and focused on trying to deploy firemen in the most effective way.

Some hours after midnight, Damrell was, however, forced to leave the frontlines when a messenger told him Mayor William Gaston wanted to meet with him at City Hall. He initially tried to ignore the summons, but soon realized he had to obey the mayor's orders. He hurried to City Hall on School Street, only a few blocks from the fire's perimeter. He walked into a room filled with about fifteen men, the gas lights flickering on their anxious faces. He looked first to Mayor Gaston, a seasoned politician who had served as mayor of Roxbury before it was annexed to Boston and was elected Boston mayor in 1870. Gaston had arrived in the city about 10:30 p.m. and had spoken to Damrell briefly on the fire lines, questioning him about his plans to save the city. The chief had outlined his strategy. But now, hours later, it seemed as if Damrell's forces were being overwhelmed.

Among the men in the room were city councilors and aldermen, including the head of the Boston Fire Committee, William Woolley, and prominent citizens, such as General Henry W. Benham, who had served in the Mexican American and Civil War and now supervised the Boston Harbor sea walls. Just arriving was William L. Burt, the city's popular and pugnacious postmaster. Burt, a Harvard-educated lawyer, had served as a Judge Advocate General through the Civil War and was given the rank of Brigadier General in 1865. Appointed postmaster of Boston by President Andrew Johnson in 1867, Burt almost immediately embarked on an ambitious building program. At that time, the post office was in the Merchants Exchange Building on State Street. Burt envisioned a grand new building that would accommodate all of Boston's future needs. That five-story structure was under construction on Congress Street between Milk and Water Streets, built from Cape Ann granite and designed in an ornate Second Empire style. A ceremony for the laying of the cornerstone had been held on October 16, 1871, and was attended by then-President Ulysses S. Grant.

Now fire was threatening to destroy the still-incomplete building. Burt was determined to prevent that from happening. Earlier that night, Burt had twice made a circuit around the fire and what he had seen told him the conflagration was beyond control. Streams from the fire engines were not reaching rooftops and sparks were leaping from one roof to the next. The current post office, he realized, might be lost. He quickly ordered that mail and valuables be packed for possible quick transfer to the city's Custom Tower building, a quarter mile away.

William L. Burt, the Boston postmaster.

Burt was an impatient man. Several times during the evening, he had gone to City Hall to find out what was being planned, only to find it dark. He demanded that it should be lit up for a meeting, telling a clerk to send for the mayor. "Boston will be another Chicago by tomorrow if nothing is done to control the fire," he declared. He then rushed back to the fire perimeter to check on the mail-packing; he was dismayed to see streets blazing without a fire engine or hose wagon in sight. He ordered postal employees to begin moving mail to the Custom Tower.

Then he returned to City Hall, where Mayor Gaston and other officials had gathered and where Chief Damrell had just arrived. The discussion began over what would prove to be the most contentious issue of the fire.

"I am here. What do you want?" Gaston asked Burt.

Burt was undeterred by Gaston's brusque manner. "Mr. Mayor, this city is burning up, the fire is beyond control. Something must be done to stop it. It needs organization instantly."

"What do you advise?" Gaston asked.

"We must blow up buildings and do it thoroughly," Burt asserted.

What Burt was suggesting was not as bizarre or unusual as it may sound to modern ears. Employing barrels of gunpowder, firemen would blow up buildings to create fire breaks that would prevent a conflagration from spreading. Fire breaks were a proven fire-fighting technique. However, blowing up buildings was a dangerous business. "To drop a building, there must be a cavity, and it should be shored to accomplish the purpose, otherwise the external walls would be simply blown out, leaving the floors and stored merchandise fully exposed and in a fit condition for a good bonfire" was how Damrell would explain it. Explosions had to be carefully planned. Fire engines had to be ready to hose down rubble to ensure that the area truly prevented flames from crossing over.

Damrell himself had been considering the use of explosives. The fire department already kept track of everywhere in the city where gunpowder was stored, so he knew it was available. Earlier in the evening, he had ordered two assistant engineers, William Green and Zenas Smith, to locate and gather a supply. He also spoke to the mayor and several aldermen about the idea when they approached him on the fire lines. The mayor assured him that the city would back him up if he chose to take this route, but he obviously had to be careful about safety. Damrell remained uneasy about the technique. While in Chicago, he had had a long conversation with General Philip Sheridan, who had coordinated Chicago's firefighting efforts and was considered that city's savior. Newspapers had lauded Sheridan for successfully employing gunpowder to create strategic fire breaks. But Sheridan told Damrell that this was not true, and that the blowing up of buildings had proved useless or had helped the fire spread.

Now, in the Boston City Hall meeting, Burt argued that gunpowder was the only recourse. "Mr. Mayor, before tomorrow morning, if you look out of that window—if the City Hall is saved, which I doubt, unless there is something done you will see [all the way] to the [ships] in the harbor."

Gaston, in later testimony, developed a kind of political amnesia about what happened next. "General Burt talked a lot," he recalled drily. Yet he was obviously concerned by Burt's apocalyptic predictions. Burt, however, remembered the conversation in detail. Gaston suggested that the explosions could cause a loss of life. Burt replied that more lives would be lost if the buildings weren't blown up. He argued that buildings should be blown in the blocks between Devonshire and Federal Streets and from the Old South Meeting House on Washington Street back to the new post office building.

"Are you ready to take charge of this?" the mayor asked.

"I am," Burt replied, without hesitation.

The exchange troubled Damrell but he feared he was running out of options. Perhaps, he thought, he could count on Burt and others to handle the explosions properly. The mayor told Burt he did not have the

DEVONSHIRE STREET LOOKING SOUTH.

Firefighters could not stop the flames on Devonshire Street. Illustration from Charles "Carleton" Coffin's *The Story of the Great Fire.*

authority to approve the blowing up of buildings by civilians—that was up to Damrell. At the mayor's direction, Damrell sat at a desk and wrote several notes giving permission for Burt and other citizens "to assist in removing items from buildings and to blow them up." He later considered this action his biggest mistake during the Great Fire.

Satisfied, Burt left, declaring he would take care of the block between Federal and Devonshire.

As the meeting broke up, Damrell went to the top of City Hall to survey the fire. He was preparing to return to the fire when General Benham pulled him aside. Benham told him he should stay at City Hall, that he was the chief director of fire response, and he should maintain a headquarters there.

"That will do, General, for the field, but it will not do in this case," Damrell replied. His place was back on the front lines.

With Assistant Engineer John Jacobs, a trusted colleague, Damrell scouted out a possible location for gunpowder. He decided to blow up a three-story building on Milk Street. He had the street cleared and he and

Jacobs hauled ten twenty-five-pound kegs of gunpowder into the building. Damrell had hoped to put the powder on the second floor, but fire was already dancing in the upper floors. Cinders were flying as thickly as flakes in a driving snowstorm. Damrell pushed a fuse into four of the kegs; he did not have time to get fuses to the others; he and Jacobs were already brushing sparks and cinders off the kegs. Damrell lit the fuses, saying to Jacobs, "If we go up, we will go together; but we will make a clean thing of this." The pair escaped barely ahead of the explosion, Damrell jumping through a window. The blast lifted up the roof, dropped it on the first floor and broke glass all around. Fire swept over the ruins, but firemen were able to douse the flames.

Damrell, acting alone, blew up another building on Batterymarch Street. This one dropped better, but because of the need to wet down the rubble, he had to order that firemen stay near the site, thus pulling them away from other locations. Gunpowder was not the answer, Damrell decided.

Explosion of Granite Stores on Congress Street, Nov. 10th, at 4 o'clock, A. M.

As captured in this illustration for the Chandler account of the fire, gunpower was ignited on Congress Street about 4:00 a.m. in an attempted to create a fire break.

Meanwhile, General Burt was busy. With two policemen, he went to Franklin Street between Federal and Devonshire, and ordered seven kegs of gunpowder to be placed in buildings. This was detonated, but the explosion only blew off the roof of one building. By now, loads of gunpowder were being brought from the Charlestown Navy Yard. Burt and his group used this to blow up buildings at different points at the northern perimeter of the fire. The building on the east side of the new post office was now on fire. Burt and his committee blew up four or five more buildings in this area, with limited success. If only he had six hundred pounds of gunpowder to destroy a building at the corner of Devonshire and Water, he was sure that the fire would have stopped there. Instead, flames spread up Lindall Street to Liberty Square. Another building was demolished at the corner of Kilby and State Streets, and Burt could see firemen gaining a toehold on the fire there. He could also see that fire was licking the walls of the new post office, but he was hopeful it could be saved. It didn't matter to him how many buildings had to be destroyed; there was no building blown up that night for which he would have given an ordinary straw hat, no matter how much the building might have cost. As for the legality of his actions, he said, "On such an occasion as that, I think no man should stop to study the law."

General Benham was also busy with gunpowder. The process was chaotic. Would-be detonators were unsure where to put the kegs of gunpowder, how much to use, and how to effectively ignite them. One man used a fuse that took eighteen minutes to burn; the fire ignited the powder long before the fuse did. An ex-alderman who helped set a charge would later say he was unsure that the explosion took down the building because "I was running for my own preservation."

Others were putting themselves at risk. Henry Lee Higginson, a prominent citizen who would later organize the Boston Symphony Orchestra, spent the first part of the night trying to fend off clients who wanted to get into the Union Safety Deposit Vaults his family owned. Later, he went to city hall to beg the mayor to order the blowing up of buildings. "I bothered the mayor almost to death, I suppose, that night," he later admitted. General Benham telegraphed nearby US Army forts; in response, a number of kegs of powder arrived at the end of Long Wharf.

The new Post Office Building, Burt's pride and joy, managed to resist destruction during the fire. BOSTON PUBLIC LIBRARY

"But there was nobody to fetch it up," Higginson recalled. "So I found a covered wagon open at the sides, got it to the end of Long Wharf, and loaded some thirty kegs of powder on it and drove up State Street, which was full of engines pumping and sparks were flying in every direction." He added, "It was a wicked thing to do, I suppose." He loaded up powder in a building next to the Shoe and Leather Bank, preparing to light the fuse if the building caught fire. Just then, Alderman Woolley arrived "as violent as he always is, I suppose, and said he would put me in jail if I didn't go away and mind my own business and let the powder alone," Higginson said. "He was very angry, and some of the firemen were very angry about it indeed." Woolley was indeed furious at the slipshod use of gunpowder.

Many citizens were cheered by the booms echoing over the city. At last! Something was being done to prevent Boston from becoming another Chicago. What many citizens did not see was how often explosions spread the fire. Moreover, some of those booms weren't caused by gunpowder.

It defies logic, but firemen and others were unable to turn off the natural gas mains that provided light to the city. When buildings burned down or were blown up, gas continued to flow. It pooled amid the rubble and ignited from flying sparks. Burt sent a messenger to the Boston Gas Company office on West Street, and even went once himself, but they couldn't find a company official who could turn off the gas flow that night.

Burt and his party set off a charge in one building. He was happy to see that the roof fell in and the entire building collapsed. As the firemen moved in to hose down the rubble, a second explosion set debris flying and flames shooting in every direction. In five minutes, the site was one mass of flame. A stream of gas "as large as my arm" poured out close to the sidewalk into the ruins, until the entire spot was aglow, Burt said. "No man could do anything under such circumstances." This experience was repeated about six times more, yet it did not satiate Burt's appetite for explosions. "If we could have got at the mains and shut off the gas, that difficulty would have been avoided," he insisted later.

By Sunday morning, Damrell had enough of gunpowder. Firemen were rushing up to him to say that buildings were being blown up in haphazard ways and explosions were spreading the fire rather than controlling it. No more explosions, he decided. He sent word via Assistant Engineer Smith that the use of gunpowder should be halted. He received word back from Alderman Woolley that one man refused to obey. Damrell sent word back by the same party to tell Woolley, "Arrest the man and lock him up until I get there, if he resists, and take the police to do it."

Woolley eagerly carried out these orders. He was dismayed by the chaotic explosions. His position was buttressed by the arrival of Smith, who told the man determined to detonate his powder that "Captain Damrell says, 'If anybody undertakes to blow up any more buildings, have them arrested, and if you can't arrest them, kill them.'"

In a scene of dark comedy, Woolley faced off with General Benham, who was seeking to blow up buildings between Kilby and Congress Streets. Benham insisted he was among those granted permission to oversee the gunpowder explosions.

"Not anymore," Woolley said.

"Who gives you such authority?" Benham demanded.

"I am the chairman of the Committee on the Fire Department, and these explosions are demoralizing the firemen," Woolley shouted.

"Do you know who I am?" Benham shouted back.

"I do not," replied the alderman.

"I am General Benham."

"I don't care if you are General Damnation. That powder is not going into the building and if you attempt to have it put in, I will have these men arrested."

"You have not the power," Benham insisted.

Woolley turned to two police officers he had brought with him. "If they undertake to put that powder in there, arrest them!"

Benham tried to plead with the officers.

"We know nobody but Alderman Woolley" they replied. "We don't know you, and we shall have to do what Mr. Woolley tells us to do."

The impasse ended with the arrival of Assistant Engineer Joseph Dunbar with orders from Damrell that explicitly said all explosions should be halted.

Burt also received this order to stop using explosives. By now, he had nearly two tons of powder on North Market Street, a ton and a half in Dock Square, and an additional ton near Kilby Street, some of which had been placed in buildings. While he likely disagreed with the decision, he followed orders and had the gunpowder removed without incident. Burt would always insist that gunpowder saved the city, but he seemed to hold no grudge against Damrell's opposition to the approach. Instead, he went out of his way to praise both Damrell and the fire service.

At about 10:00 a.m. on Sunday, Damrell arrived at the new post office building to check the situation there. Burt and Damrell both climbed into the building to check on the condition of the interior. Woolley also appeared and directed firefighters to pour water into the building. "No complaint can certainly be made of any amount of efficiency and daring of the Fire Department there. They obeyed orders and assumed risks of life and limb that were only justified by the immense amount of valuable property exposed to destruction," Burt later said. The new post office building would suffer great damage to the interior, but it would stand, he added. "It was like a fortification. The engines could fall back there, knowing that they could stay there and would not have to move. Everything about the building was reliable."

Other victories against the Fire Fiend came with determination and ingenuity. The employees of Hovey's department store managed to rescue their building on Summer Street. Perhaps their devotion was a legacy of the store's original owner Charles Fox Hovey, a progressive who put his principles into practice. Hovey had run various businesses and partnerships since the 1840s, finally setting up a general goods store on Summer Street. Hovey pioneered the use of the one-price system in retail; previously clerks used bartering techniques to talk up quality (and hence prices). Hovey discarded that practice for the approach represented by his slogan, "A standard good at a standard price." He was also an abolitionist who had supported William Lloyd Garrison's Anti-Slavery Society, and he believed in profit-sharing with employees. He had died in 1859, but his relatives still ran the business at the time of the Great Fire. Now his employees repaid his faith.

They wet down carpets and blankets and spread them over the roof and over the windows. They had to keep replacing them with new ones, using trickles of water from faltering faucets. One fire company assisted by bringing a hose to the upper floors for water. As the fire roared up Summer Street, taking down Trinity Church just across the street, the employees remained at their posts, beating away sparks and debris with the wet cloth. According to one source, the Quincy Fire Department chief, a buyer for Hovey's, helped direct the operation. Through their actions, the employees saved the store even as destruction rained around them. "If the merchants of Boston who have suffered would have done the same, the desolation of this morning would not be so great," Chief Damrell wrote in a letter of commendation for the employees' herculean efforts.

As the sun rose on Sunday morning, Boston citizens wavered between anxiety and outright panic. There were reports that carloads of "roughs

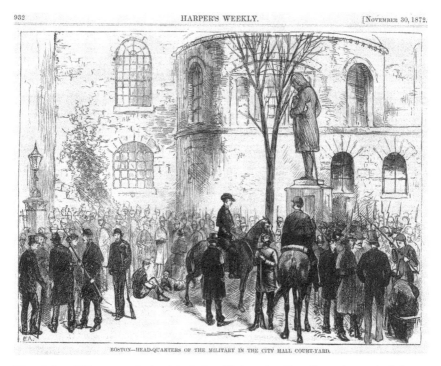

932   HARPER'S WEEKLY.   [NOVEMBER 30, 1872.

BOSTON—HEAD-QUARTERS OF THE MILITARY IN THE CITY HALL COURT-YARD.

The state militia was called out to help with keeping the city under control; here soldiers are shown at a temporary headquarters outside Boston City Hall. From *Harper's Weekly*, November 30, 1872.

and thieves" from New York City were coming by train to loot the devastated city and had cleaned out the saloons on the stops along the way to Boston. The *Boston Traveler* subsequently reported that these would-be looters had left town discouraged. The trip had been unprofitable due to the alertness of the militia, which had been called in, and the Boston Police Department. Of Boston's 522 police officers, 400 were called out to be on the lines during the fire. They had made dozens of arrests for looting; many of the cases proved to be merchants rescuing items or clerks sent to recover what they could from burning buildings. "I never saw a fire like this, where there was so much excitement," said Boston Police Chief Edward Savage. In the wake of reports of rail-riding looters, Savage organized a cadre of officers to meet the incoming train. The cars were mostly empty and the police took in only six men. "I asked, 'Where are the rest?' They said, 'Got sea-sick, and went home.' I have no question but [that] there was a large number of them that came as far as Worcester; but they didn't come here. If they had, we should have had some fun with them."

Eighteen-year-old Grace Revere, of the famed Paul Revere clan, feared the worst, writing a friend in Europe, "Do you realize that is going on here and what a state of awe and horror we are in? So many roughs have arrived from New York that every precaution is being taken for personal safety. It is dreadful to think how many beautiful things have been stolen by this [sic] horrid people and it is still more dreadful to feel that our house may be broken into during the night." Grace also repeated the false rumor that two men were caught during the night setting fires and were hanged from a lamp post, "which seems too small a punishment for such scamps."

By Sunday midmorning, the fire had decimated about six wharves and ignited sheds that would smolder for months. It had reached Liberty Square to the northeast and was pushing toward State Street and the Fort Hill area. On its southwest flank, it was moving toward Washington Street.

Damrell prepared for a final stand. He determined that the firestorm currents had a velocity of twenty to thirty miles per hour and were rushing to fill a vacuum created at the center of the fire, where oxygen had been depleted. This drew heat from outward boundaries into the interior. He

BOSTON—WASHINGTON STREET, LOOKING TOWARD THE "OLD SOUTH CHURCH" FROM SUMMER STREET.
FROM A PHOTOGRAPH BY J. A. WHIPPLE, BOSTON.—[SEE NEXT PAGE.]

A view of the fire from the west side of Washington Street shows the Old South Meeting House and the ruins of the Boston Transit building. From *Harper's Weekly*, November 30, 1872.

concluded that Washington, Milk, Devonshire, State, and Broad Streets would be the best points from which to operate. The heat would not be as great there and firemen could hold their positions. Water appeared to be more abundant there as well. He ordered that engines be massed at points along these streets. Damrell refused to consider the blowing up of any more buildings; he believed the fire could be stopped there. With a massive show of force from more than twenty-five steamers, his tactics seemed to be working.

But one significant landmark in the city appeared to be doomed.

CHAPTER 9

The Fire That Would Not Die

In many respects . . . this second fire was the most frightening to Bos-
ton. Saturday night, complacency had given way to panic. Sunday
night seemed to show that all Boston was doomed to the crucible of fire.
—DIANE RUDNICK
BOSTON AND THE FIRE OF 1872:
THE STILLBORN PHOENIX, 1971

THE OLD SOUTH MEETING HOUSE ON WASHINGTON STREET IS ONE OF the oldest buildings in Boston and the very symbol of the American Revolution. The Old South was built as a Puritan meeting house in 1729. Its congregation included African American poet Phillis Wheatley; revolutionary firebrand Samuel Adams; William Dawes, who rode with Paul Revere to Lexington in 1775; and the young Benjamin Franklin and his family. In a meeting there in December 1773, the Boston Tea Party was planned. As revenge, the British later used the building as a stable during the Revolutionary War. It was finally restored in 1783 and became a congregation once again. The steeple was a distinctive landmark of the Boston skyline and its location in the commercial district was a reminder of the days when the area was filled with homes.

Now, as the clock in the church tower struck the time on Sunday morning, many thought they might never hear that sound again. The Fire Fiend was approaching from the east, and Washington Street seemed destined for burning. "Sober citizens, who had borne the loss of their own fortunes without a word, were seen absolutely frantic with distress as the conflagration approached this venerable pile," according to the *Chicago Tribune.*

General Burt was approached three times by people about blowing up the Old South. He told them it was not necessary, that the fire could be stopped there. That seemed increasingly unlikely. But help would come from an unexpected place.

About five hours earlier, Portsmouth, New Hampshire, Mayor Thomas E.O. Marvin was aroused from sleep by a knock at his door. A policeman stood on his doorstep with a telegram that read: "Fire in Boston beyond our control. Come immediately to our aid."

Marvin wrote on the back: "Coming with steam fire engine and forty veteran firemen."

Called by the ringing of church bells, firemen from Portsmouth's Engine Company 3, with Marvin, gathered and loaded their Amoskeag fire engine on a flatbed railcar and set off for Boston. The company was very proud of its engine, purchased barely two years earlier from the Amoskeag Machine Company's factory in Manchester. "The engine is of a superior model and makes a fine appearance, weighing about 5,000 pounds, having a double cylinder, with extra composition cylinders to use in place of iron ones when salt water is to be used, for which $200 extra was paid, the whole cost being $4000.00. The fairy-like hose carriage costing $600 is a specimen of work, endowed, we should say, with 'the power of endurance' of the hardest usage," the *Portsmouth Journal of Literature and Politics* reported. It was named for the famous USS *Kearsarge*, a Mohican-Class sloop-of-War, built and launched at the Portsmouth Naval Shipyard.

In Marvin's recollection, the light from the conflagration raging in Boston could be seen as the train chugged southward. Within two hours, the Kearsarge was being unloaded at the Causeway Rail Station and dragged toward the fire. The company set their hoses in a reservoir and took up a station near Washington and Milk Streets. Streams from nearby engines were falling short of the roofs of the nearby buildings, including the *Transcript* building. Recalled William S. Hazen, the clerk of Portsmouth Engine Number Three: "Our chief gave us the order to reach the roof with our stream which we did causing a round of cheers to rend the air from the Boston firemen and citizens." Yet the heat was so fierce that the water often turned to steam, reflecting the colors of the rainbow

FRANK LESLIE'S
ILLUSTRATED
NEWSPAPER

No. 896—Vol. XXXV.]   NEW YORK, NOVEMBER 30, 1872.   [Price, 10 Cents.

THE GREAT FIRE IN BOSTON.—THE DESPERATE EFFORTS OF THE FIREMEN AND CITIZENS TO SAVE THE OLD SOUTH CHURCH.
From a Sketch by J. N. Hyde.—See Page 187.

The Old South Meeting House, one of the city's most historical buildings, nearly succumbed to the fire but a concerted effort including help from outside fire companies, saved the church. From front page of *Frank Leslie's Illustrated Newspaper*, November 30, 1872.

THE OLD SOUTH DEFYING THE FLAMES.

The fight to save the Old South from Charles Coffin's book on the fire.

John W. Black captured firemen trying to wet down coal on a Boston Harbor dock. BOSTON PUBLIC LIBRARY

in the sunlight. The *Transcript* building collapsed, showering firebrands on the Old South roof and burying three firemen from Worcester. The Portsmouth men sent water streaming on the heated piles of brick, and one jumped into the chaos to try to pull out the Worcester men. He succeeded, but one of the injured men died a few hours later. For hours, the men played water on the Old South, drenching the structure but keeping it intact. At about 3:30 p.m. fire was deemed out. Marvin hastened to the church's basement, where a venerable white-haired sexton had remained heroically at his post, guarding the vestibule doors. He told the sexton the fire was out and the church was saved. "A more fervent 'Thank God' never issued from human lips than the old sexton uttered when he heard the glad tidings," Marvin said later.

With the rescue of the Old South and the success of the line of fire engines near the new post office building, the fire was deemed under control by late Sunday afternoon. But it was not actually extinguished.

"Enormous piles of lumber, leather, dry goods, and other combustible material still streamed with fire and rolled up vast columns of smoke, seemingly filling the dome of heaven with cloudy peaks and cliffs," Conwell wrote. "All that dreary Sunday night, feverish flushes of firelight discolored the sky; and occasionally some rubbish heap would burst and flare with a magnesian glow, making igneous shadows on the landscape fifty miles away."

Fire companies were still arriving from Connecticut and Maine. Damrell opted to keep them in the city to relieve exhausted firemen from Boston and other cities. Firemen continued to pour water on hot spots, but the Fire Fiend seemed to finally be vanquished.

Until it wasn't.

Late on Sunday night, reporter Sylvester Baxter was in the *Advertiser's* office on State Street, trying to write his stories, when the fire alarm sounded. A second. A third. He sped to the *Advertiser's* roof, and to his horror, saw flames rising to the south near the corner of Summer and Washington Streets. When he returned to the newsroom, he could not speak, the blood draining from his face. At last, he was able to spit out, "The fire has broken out again. Terribly. Crossed Washington Street. It will surely get here."

Everyone who has watched a horror movie knows there are typically at least two endings: one when everyone thinks the monster is dead and then, usually a few minutes later, another when the monster rises and has to be killed all over again. So it was with the Fire Fiend.

Although the fire was deemed under control on Sunday afternoon, gas continued to flow out of broken mains. The Boston Gas Company had no way of turning off the gas street by street and the gas was pooling amid the rubble. About midnight, four explosions on Summer Street near the popular Shreve, Crump and Low jewelry and gift store rattled an already frantic city. Iron manhole covers in that district went sailing through the air like so many autumn leaves, and once again Boston was on fire. An entire block of stores, which had successfully resisted all advances of the Fire Fiend up to this time, ignited.

This second fire quickly spread from the corner of Summer and Washington Streets. Fire companies from New Haven and Norwich, Connecticut,

This extraordinary photo by James Wallace Black was likely taken on Washington Street on November 10, even before the fire was officially under control. A smoking fire engine can be seen at the base of the Old South. DIGITAL COMMONWEALTH

who had only recently arrived found themselves plunged in a fierce battle zone. A panicked woman leaped to her death from an upper-story window; her mother was found dead inside the building. People again swarmed

THE OUTSIDE AID COMING

An illustration from the December 7, 1872, *Harper's Weekly* depicts fire engines from outside Boston being pulled to the fire through Boston's streets.

the streets, and merchants on West and Winter Streets and Temple Place frantically tried to move their goods, blocking thoroughfares in their mad endeavors. With the aid of the out-of-town men and equipment, firemen battled this new blaze for four hours. Finally, the gas flow was cut when the Boston Gas Company turned off all the gas mains in the city. With the help of the out-of-town firemen, the Fire Fiend was rousted.

. Receipt

Crawford Branch
410-887-1919
www.bcpl.info

Tuesday, August 2, 2022 3:11:50 PM
69121

Item: 31183210277794
Title: Patton's payback : the battle of El Guett
ar and General Patton's rise to glory
Call no.: 940.5423 M
Due: 8/23/2022

Item: 31183206898535
Title: The Great Boston Fire : an inferno that n
early incinerated the city
Call no.: 974.461 S
Due: 8/23/2022

Total items: 2

You just saved $54.95 by using your
library today.

Free to Be All In
Late fees no longer
assessed for overdue items
Ask for details or visit bcpl.info

www.bcpl.info
Shelf Help 410-494-9063

Fed by dispatches from its reporters on scene and in New York, the *New York Sun* dedicated nearly its entire front page of November 12 to Boston's fire, complete with a map of the Burnt District. One unnamed scribe described what he saw on the streets:

> *As I write. I hear the shriek of fire engine whistles alternating with the roll of drums which come from the numerous bodies of troops patrolling the streets. Cavalry, with draw sabers are met at every turn and if the city doesn't pull through without dropping into confusion it won't be for want of active precautions. In the streets, the newsboys keep up an incessant shouting of extras which appear at short intervals, which is unpleasant. People mechanically turn their eyes toward the burnt*

A dramatic depiction of the ruins of Washington Street, printed in the November 30, 1872, *Illustrated London News.*

district, looking with terror upon the flaming banners, which is still threatening waves over the city.

Still, the reporter added, "That the Old South Church escaped the flames is a source of joy to everybody and the people look fondly up to it when the clock strikes the hour."

Grace Revere could not be comforted. "We have only candles and no streetlamps and it is altogether so melancholy that I should like to have a good cry," she wrote. By Tuesday, "I slept with one eye open and my stockings on but hope that we will have a better night tonight."

One of the difficulties in writing a history of the fire is that so many contemporary accounts focus on lurid descriptions and hearsay. Remarkably, an enterprising reporter for the *New York Sun* managed to get one of the most dramatic and complete eyewitness accounts from the fire while in New York. He met trains coming in from Boston, hoping to interview an arriving Bostonian about the fire, and accosted Barney O'Neil of Spaulding & Company. O'Neil was a tall man with a commanding dignified air, a pleasant face, and long heavy blonde whiskers. He wore a heavy overcoat and brown kid gloves and carried a small valise in his hand. Holding up the valise and smiling, he said, "This is all there is left of Spaulding & Co. of Boston."

"Are you Mr. Spaulding?" the reporter asked.

"No, I am the 'co.' My name is Barney O'Neil."

The reporter asked whether O'Neil could provide an intelligent story on the fire.

"Now, my dear fellow, don't talk about intelligence in a case of this kind. Men can't be intelligent or stop to calculate causes and effects when they see their all reduced to ashes."

O'Neil had been at his home in Somerville, outside Boston, when, he said, "My little boy rushed in the room and cried 'Oh, Pa, come and see, Boston is on fire?'" O'Neil went outside and saw that the night sky was bright scarlet. He had been burned out before, and in fifteen minutes he was at his store at 67 Congress Street near Milk Street, where he met other men from his company.

"We have two safes belonging to the firm . . . and we went to work to remove [one]. . . . We managed to get it as far as the door when a heavy sound smote upon our ears. Every window in the building was shattered and the broken glass fell crashing about it. They had blown up the large granite building on the corner of Milk Street. This shock frightened us. I am an old Californian, and it takes a good deal to scare me, but I was as much frightened as the rest. We thought only of saving our own lives and hurried from the building. It was well that we did. Before we had gone ten rods, the flames swept down upon the place we had deserted like an avalanche. They fairly licked it out of existence. It melted like so much lead."

O'Neil told the reporter that the burned area might be small in comparison to Chicago, "but my dear fellow every acre represented millions. I don't believe $100 million will cover the real estate losses and the value of stock destroyed by the fire and water will foot up millions more. That beautiful curve forming Winthrop Square contained the most magnificent buildings in Boston. They were all fireproof but they melted down in an incredibly short time. . . . You can form some notion of the extreme intensity of the heat when I tell you that thousands of tons of coal stored at the Hartford and Erie Depot were burning this morning and actually flowed about like liquid fire."

O'Neil felt obligated to defend Boston's firefighters. Various observers had given conflicting reports about firemen joining the other tipplers in the streets. "I suppose your reporters will write letters about 'The Drunken Men in Boston.' The city is full of drunken men, but I tell you men who were in the streets wading through dirty water and suffering from fervent heat all night and all day need something to keep them up. The excitement of a scene like that cannot be borne by ordinary men without something the way of stimulants."

For a man who had seen his business go up in flames as he ran for his life, O'Neil was remarkably chipper. "The people will rather be gainers than losers by the fire," he told the *Sun* reporter. "They will have worked all winter for, of course, Boston is to be rebuilt and this time we mean to have straight and wide streets. The wealthy man has lost his property and the workingman, so far as I can see, is going to reap the benefit of it.

"I did not save a cent's worth myself. But as I said before, I have been flooded, 'earthquaked,' and burned out. I have risen above calamity before and I mean to triumph again. I have come on here to get all I can out of our insurance and then we shall set up again. The firm of Spaulding & Co. isn't dead yet."

O'Neil took his leave of the *Sun* reporter and headed into the city.

Biddeford fireman James E. Gowan went home to Maine with a souvenir. The proprietors of Jordan Marsh saw the freezing conditions of the firemen on the front line and gave each of them a big, puffy quilt. "Every man brought the quilt he received home with him," Gowan told a newspaper in the early 1900s. "I have mine and I would not take $100 for it."

On Monday, Sylvester Baxter finished writing his stories. "Up to that time, I had always felt the delight of the average boy in the presence of a fire," he would later say. "But November 9, 1872, sickened me of fires. I never wanted to see another."

CHAPTER 10

Seeing Double

Among the incidents of the day, it may be mentioned that the pho-
tographers appeared with their apparatus and selected with artistic
judgment points of view for the most picturesque representations of
the scene of desolation. The early appearance of stereoscopic views of
peculiar interest may be predicted.
—*BOSTON GLOBE*, NOVEMBER 13, 1872

AS THE SUN ROSE OVER A WRECKED AND SMOLDERING BOSTON ON MON-
day, November 11, John Payson Soule wasted no time rejoicing that his
Washington Street photography studio had escaped the fire, albeit barely.
He gathered his equipment, camera, chemicals, and plates, packed them
into a small wagon covered with dark cloth, and rushed out into still-
smoking streets. There was history to record, of course, but more important, there was money to be made.

Soule knew he had a little time and a lot of ground to cover. The forty-
four-year-old, one of Boston's foremost photographers, had considerable
experience with the technology of exposing plates doused with chemicals
to capture images. He faced many challenges, first and foremost the issue
of light. At that time in November, there was only enough sunlight for
making photos from about 11:00 a.m. to 3:00 p.m. Even then, a layer of
smoke hung over the city, the sky was overcast, and it would rain later that
night. Soule also had to contend with militia assembled throughout what
would soon be called the Burnt District to protect against looting. He
would have to work quickly and efficiently.

Fortunately, he didn't need to travel far to get what he wanted: evocative images of once- magnificent buildings and streets transformed into grotesque ruins and twisted remnants. He set up his equipment for his first shots just blocks from his studio. Using "wet-plate" photography, Soule covered a plane of glass with a syrupy substance called collodion, dipped it into silver nitrate, and loaded it into his camera, where he exposed it to light from twenty seconds to five minutes. Then, before the plate fully dried, he pulled it out, transferred it to the "dark room" in his wagon, and used more chemicals to develop and fix the image. This process took about fifteen minutes. If all went well, he would have a glass negative that could be used to make prints on paper coated with albumen, which was egg white with chloride. It was a cumbersome process and something could go wrong at every step.

Soule first set up his camera on Washington Street to record the site of Fowle, Torrey & Company's destroyed carpet warehouse. Then he positioned his equipment for shots up Milk Street. He lingered at the corner with Summer Street to get multiple angles of the wrecked Trinity Church. He worked until he lost light. The next day and the next, Soule exposed hundreds of plates along Summer, High, Pearl, Milk, and Washington Streets, tracing the perimeter of the Burnt District.

Soule was joined by more than two dozen other photographers, all moving through the ravaged business district. Prominent among them was the nationally known James Wallace Black, who had managed to get some of the first aerial shots of Boston by riding in a balloon above the city. Despite narrowly escaping being burned out of his own studio on Washington Street, he had ventured out on Sunday afternoon, when the fire was not yet contained, and captured a photo of what may have been the New Hampshire steam engine, *Kearsarge*, still smoking, near the Old South Meeting House. He was making negatives even as the fire burned dangerously close to his studio. "I consider myself a fortunate individual to escape as I have," he admitted. "I have plenty of glass [the glasses plates] and a strong will to do anything, and what more can be desired?" Other photographers, including John Adams Whipple, who had been the first official class photographer for Harvard from 1852 to 1859, Charles Pollock, and J.S. Moulton mingled with the

Samples of stereographic cards of the Great Boston Fire sold via eBay.
AUTHOR'S COLLECTION

Samples of stereographic cards of the Great Boston Fire sold via eBay. AUTHOR'S COLLECTION

firemen, onlookers, business owners, and militia in the hunt to record the most horrific and awe-inspiring images of Boston's ruination.

I have—via the immense yard sale that is eBay—one of John Soule's photographs. It's actually two images of the same scene, set side-by-side on a 7- by 3-inch rectangle of stiff cardboard with a sickly yellow border. According to the caption, this represents the "Effects of Fire on Granite Walls, Pearl Street." It is easy to see why Soule was fascinated by this scene. It shows a burnt-out façade of an eviscerated building, like flesh stripped from bones. What remains of the building loops across the frame in a fluid series of arches. Heaps of boulders lie at the base. Beyond the arches, you can glimpse outlines of battered buildings. The entire effect is that of a ruin left by an ancient civilization—Roman, perhaps, or Aztec. Soule apparently exposed at least six plates of this scene, which attracted other photographers as well. After nearly 150 years, the Soule photo has faded to a sepia tint; details are almost lost. Yet it still "works."

I slip the Soule card between two wire loops into another of my eBay purchases, a 1904 contraption with a lens set in an etched tin frame and placed on a long narrow piece of polished wood. I press my face against the viewing lens and look at the card. The image acquires depth. I can almost make out the rivulets of melted granite, and the buildings in the distance are ghostly shadows, misty pockets of doom. The card lacks the clarity and color of the View-Masters of my youth, but I feel I'm peering back in time, at what passed for virtual reality in the nineteenth century.

That was one of the reasons Soule and dozens of other photographers rushed to the fire. They wanted photos they could print and mount, to be sure, but they also wanted to use those images for a special nineteenth-century pastime: stereography. In the parlors of homes in Boston, New York, London, and other cities, people passed around stenographic cards with images of European castles or Egyptian pyramids or pastoral valleys and towering mountains. The 3D effect was, to the Victorian eye, magical. Today, the cards seem rather quaint. They, along with the original photos from which they were produced, are part of the legacy of the Great Boston Fire.

No photograph of the actual fire exists; there was not enough light, and photography then required subjects to remain still during exposures.

View from corner Washington & Bromfield Sts. By Whipple.

A number of photographers managed to put together panoramic views of the fire which were quite popular sales item. This photo was taken by John Adams Whipple and is in the collection of the Boston Public Library.

But photographs of its aftermath reveal the power of the Fire Fiend. "Each street had a story to tell and Boston's photographers were extremely effective in providing the vehicle for its telling," Michael J. Novak wrote in his 1992 book *Photography and the Great Boston Fire of November 1872*, in which he analyzed hundreds of fire-scene photographs and meticulously cataloged the work of the twenty-five photographers who reconnoitered Boston's desolated streets. The demand for their work was huge.

"For the past week I have had hardly time to take a breath, such has been the call for photographs of the burnt district," Black told a photography magazine of the era. "I have made about one hundred and fifty negatives of different portions, some of which are very artistic." In a technical feat that amazed Bostonians, Black, Soule, and Whipple went to the top of extant buildings on Washington Street and other locations to create photographic panoramas of the massive ruins; their efforts to capture the wasteland remain breathtaking today.

Photographers recorded fire engines still smoking, firefighters posed against rubble, and the defiant signs of merchants marking the locations of where their businesses had stood. The ruins "have been photographed from every point of view, and nothing is more impressive or more picturesque in the ruins of ancient cities," William Lloyd Garrison wrote. What was left of Trinity Church was a popular subject; Oliver Wendell Holmes Sr. would dryly write "Trinity Church, its tower standing, its walls partly fallen [is] more imposing as a ruin than it ever was in its best estate."

The ruins of the Great Boston Fire were an irresistible draw for photographers who tried to capture as much devastation as they could. BOSTON PUBLIC LIBRARY

Boston's photographers expected a huge demand for scenes of the fire, either as stenographs or printed photos. Novak has calculated that more than 750 different images for stereograph, albumen prints, or panoramas were published or offered for sale after the fire. It was a lively market. Chicago photographers had rebuilt their trade by selling stereographs of their city's destruction the previous year, according to Novak. Soule ended up publishing at least 111 views of the fire. "This represented a Herculean effort on Soule's part involving both the time it took to amass this many plates and the expense of combining these views with quality custom card stock," Novak wrote. Black took nearly 150 photos and at least 131 different views were offered for sale. These photographs were the first of their kind, according to Novak. While plenty of photographs had been taken of the Chicago fire, those images lacked the dynamic, immediate nature of the Boston pictures. "Smoke, people, fire engines, and a sense of activity make the Boston Fire photographs the first examples of As-It-Is-Happening News photography," he wrote.

One happy owner of a fire photo was fire buff William Lloyd Garrison. Garrison's oldest son and namesake gave his father one of Black's Great Fire panoramas, handsomely framed as a "New Year's Remembrance." "It is more than four feet and a half wide and gives a vivid impression at a glance of the terrible devastation caused by that calamity," Garrison wrote his second son, Wendell Phillips Garrison with great satisfaction. "It is a picture that will possess historic interest and worth preserving to a late day."

Black, a talented landscape photographer, applied the same skills to his fire-scene photos. Stephen Robert Edidin, who wrote a monograph to accompany an exhibit of Black's photos at the Boston Athenaeum in 1977, sees another force at work in Black's output: "moralization." "Perhaps part of the power of Black's photographs stem from his realization that the Great Fire in Boston stripped away this deceptive veneer of a civilization," he wrote. As in Percy Bysshe Shelley's 1817 poem "Ozymandias," in which below the shattered visage of a "King of Kings" is written "Look on my Works ye Mighty, and despair," Black's photos mock the smugness of Boston's character.

Which is why I initially wondered who—aside from the apocalyptic-minded Garrison—would want to look at images of terrible, awful destruction as a form of entertainment via stereographic cards? That moment of naivete passed quickly; it took just a second to recall all the scenes of annihilation that have inspired Hollywood and filled movie theaters since King Kong first wrecked New York. Nineteenth-century entertainment was not that different. Disasters, fires, floods, and train wrecks were popular subjects for photographers of that era and fueled the public's appetite for stereographic images.

The principle of using double images to create a sense of depth was first observed in 1838. About a decade later scientist David Brewster crafted a handheld that device you could raise to your eyes, insert a card with two images of the same subject, and get a 3D effect—virtual reality, at least from the Victorian viewpoint. Photography had just recently been invented, which meant that the new stereoscope could create vivid images captured from real life. Brewster's design was an immediate hit.

In a June 1859 article in the *Atlantic*, Oliver Wendell Holmes Sr. (yes, him again) gushed rapturously over the beauty and power of the stereoscope. "The first effect of looking at a good photograph through the stereoscope is a surprise such as no painting ever produced. The mind feels its way into the very depths of the picture. The scraggy branches of a tree in the foreground run out at us as if they would scratch our eyes out. The elbow of a figure stands forth so as to make us almost uncomfortable. Then there is such a frightful amount of detail, that we have the same sense of infinite complexity which Nature gives us." The infatuated Holmes collected hundreds of images that he compared in value to his treasured volumes of poetry. Ever a tinkerer, Holmes designed a simpler stereoscope that could be made cheaply; because he didn't patent it, this created an American stenography boom. The craze would last for sixty years.

So, it wasn't just artistry or photojournalism that motivated Soule, Black, and others. They wanted scenes of destruction—the more terrible, the better. It would be hard to estimate just how many stereoscopic cards of the Great Boston Fire were produced, but even after 150 years, they are not a particularly rare or expensive item on eBay. I have purchased a number of them, including four from Soule. The cards are faded and dingy, but they hold a strange fascination for me. I have frequently walked the areas they depict, Pearl Street, Washington Street, Summer Street and High Street. (I worked on High Street for my first job in Boston.) There is today no trace—not a shred of evidence—of what Soule's camera captured in 1872.

The public can readily see many of the Great Fire photos and stereographic cards through Boston Public Library's Flickr site and other online sources. Viewed via a computer screen, the images offer a crisp clarity and dispassionate viewpoint that never fails to startle. Like so many photos of destruction—of Hiroshima, of the World Trade Center on September 11, 2001, of pitiless tsunamis and relentless hurricanes— photographs of Boston's Burnt District represent a visual history, a stark reminder of the city's narrow escape and a visceral reminder of what can happen when foresight fails.

While the fire photographs were stunning, the readers of newspapers and magazines around the world at the time never saw them. At least, not directly. And yet the country and Europe were able to experience the wrenching gut-punch of the Athens of America in flames via the popularity of illustrated newspapers, which matched words with sumptuous pictures. The technology to reproduce photos for the mass media did not then exist, so when photographers sent their fire-scene images to these publications, they were quickly turned into illustrations. In this way, these black-and-white drawings, some by the most famous illustrators of the day, conveyed Boston's near-annihilation to the rest of the world.

Illustrated news magazines were widely read during the 1870s. The trend began in the 1840s, when the *Illustrated London News* started using wood-block engravings to reproduce drawings and detailed illustrations for its paper. This was followed in the US in 1855 by *Frank Leslie's Illustrated Newspaper* and two years later by *Harper's Weekly*, billed as the "Journal of Civilization." These periodicals hired staff and freelance artists to be "on scene" and create sketches or create an illustration from a photograph. These would then be turned into wood-block engravings. To expedite the process, large engravings would be divided into small blocks so that multiple artists could work on the same illustration simultaneously.

Harper's Weekly helped launch the career of famed political cartoonist Thomas Nast, who popularized the elephant and the donkey as symbols for the Republican and Democratic Parties. The magazine also employed artists and illustrators such as Paul Frenzeny, Edwin Austin Abbey, and Charles Stanley Reinhart as quick sketch professionals to depict current events. In *Harper's Weekly* editions dated November 30 and December 7, these artists did what photographers could not do—document the Fire Fiend in action. A full-page illustration, inspired by a John Adams Whipple photo, shows the fire decimating Washington Street, the smoke and flames dwarfing the valiant fire engines amidst a throng of onlookers. Another *Harper's* sketch shows the military forcing back crowds, and another conveys the frantic efforts of merchants to move their goods, as well as the arrests of tough-looking looters. It's hard to determine which of the artists, if any, were at the scene, and many of the illustrations are not signed.

A series of illustrations attributed to "Paul Frenzeny's sketch-book" does seem to have been drawn from observation. They show firemen sending out streams of water behind barricades, out-of-town fire engines arriving, exhausted firemen collapsed on rubble, boys selling relics of the fire, and women in bustles and men in top hats strolling through the ruins. Frenzeny was an accomplished artist with a taste for adventure. Born in France in the 1840s, he served in Maximilian's French army in Mexico. After Maximilian's execution in 1867, Frenzeny came to New York City and took art lessons. He found work with *Harper's* and may have been in Boston—or have been sent to Boston—to cover the fire.

Thomas Nast also contributed a fire illustration: a highly romantic image, titled "Columbia lay aside her laurels to mourn at the burning of her birth-place." The Fire Fiend, depicted as a topless, snake-haired Medusa, glares as she sweeps over a scorched landscape. *Harpers* devoted an entire "double truck," or two full pages, for an illustrated bird's-eye view of Boston, which shows the Burnt District. This was based on a lithograph produced by the famed printmaking firm of Currier and Ives, which produced a very popular colored print of the fire drawn from the perspective of a ship in the harbor. The battle for the Old South graced the front page of *Frank Leslie's Illustrated Newspaper* of November 30, and the *London Illustrated News* published three remarkable detailed illustrations of the ruins based on Black's photos, which arrived by mail steamer.

One of the fire's most famous images and perhaps the most heroic portrayal ever of a nineteenth-century firefighter appeared on *Harper's* November 30 front page. It was drawn by Reinhart, a Pittsburgh native who studied art in France and became known as one of the country's most versatile illustrators, adept at both characterizations and scenery. (Willa Cather's 1904 short story, "The Sculptor's Funeral," may have been inspired by Reinhart.) He was among *Harper's* regular cadre of illustrators, and his depiction of the Great Boston Fire shows six firemen in a life-or-death struggle with an inferno. Two men grasp a hose that snakes like a python around them. One faces the viewer, fear evident in his countenance. The image's focal point is the calm face of a burly, mustachioed

COLUMBIA LAYS ASIDE HER LAURELS TO MOURN AT THE BURNING OF HER BIRTH-PLACE.

Cartoonist Thomas Nast put aside politics to draw this dramatic illustration to reflect how the nation mourned what had happened to Boston. From *Harper's Weekly*, November 30, 1872.

fireman, eyes resolute with a steel, cool detachment as he directs a stream of water. It is possible—although not likely—that Reinhart witnessed this scene; more likely he created it from imagination.

Imagined or not, these illustrations, coupled with the photos, showed a shocked world how Boston had become a second Chicago.

CHAPTER 11

"We Are Burnt Out"

All the street lines were utterly obliterated by the debris, and many a merchant found it impossible to determine precisely where he had been doing business. But the fire has caused no paralysis or despondency. Our citizens are full of hope, courage, and determination, and the work of restoration is going on with cheering alacrity.

—WILLIAM LLOYD GARRISON

THE OWNER AND EMPLOYEES OF E. B. HULL GATHERED AROUND THE company's safe, which had lain eighteen hours in a solid bed of fire and was still hot to the touch. They gingerly opened it. To their surprise and utter relief, they found their books and papers intact. Other merchants were not so lucky. They opened their safes to find only ash, or in the case of E. C. Dyer of Devonshire Street, a quantity of silver and gold coins welded together, the silver turned completely black and the gold disfigured.

For every fortunate soul, another merchant faced ruin. Almost immediately after the fire was brought under control, Boston started counting the losses, even as firemen continued to wet hot spots, such as a coal pile on a wharf that would burn for days. More than a thousand businesses were burned out of their locations. About sixty-five acres were scorched and 776 buildings damaged beyond repair. The total cost of the property and the contents lost was estimated to be more than $75 million, about $1.6 billion in today's dollars. This was 10 to 11 percent of the total assessed value of all Boston real estate and personal property. About seventy dwellings on Purchase Street were ruined and hundreds were

OPENING SAFES—THE BOOKS ALL RIGHT.

Many businessmen opened safes to find to their surprise and delight important documents intact. Others were not so lucky. From *Harper's Weekly*, November 30, 1872.

A ghostly remnant of a building captured by John W. Black. BOSTON PUBLIC
LIBRARY

left homeless. Due to its loss of life and total acreage, Chicago's fire was clearly more terrible, yet Boston's fire is considered to have been more costly per acre.

In his book on the fire, Frank E. Frothingham listed by street all the businesses affected and their losses; his accounting ran sixty pages. Wholesale dry-goods businesses, clothing houses, and the shops of boot, hide and leather dealers were smoking ash. All the domestic wool in the city was incinerated. The Hartford and Erie railroad station was consumed. Seven bank buildings were destroyed. The freight schooner *Louisa Frazer* was engulfed in flames while docked at a wharf. The city's publishing industry took a huge hit. Two newspapers, the *Transcript* and the *Pilot*, the magazines *Saturday Evening Gazette* and *American Homes,* and about a half dozen other publications lost their headquarters. Block after block were now only piles of debris, obliterating streets lines and other landmarks. "We are burnt out," was the frequent refrain of the merchant and shopkeeper. Reporter Baxter prowled the rubble for information, thanking his stars that he had a gold-stamped pass from the Common

Many enterprising merchants managed to locate the site of their old businesses and direct customers to new temporary sites. BOSTON PUBLIC LIBRARY

Council to get past the militia lines stationed on the border of the Burnt District. He ruined a pair of shoes clambering over the still-hot ruins and nearly blistered his feet.

Some losses could not be measured in dollars. The Old South was saved, but Trinity Church was damaged beyond repair. The old Post Office Building was gone; places like Merchants Hall and the Beebe Block were fit only for disaster-landscape photography. The area's warehouses and studios had stored the collections of wealthy Bostonians. Augustus Thorndike Perkins, an expert on the works of painter John Singleton Copley, took it upon himself to meticulously chronicle the losses to "literature and the fine art" for the New England Historic Genealogical Society. His tally included paintings and portraits by Copley and other artists, numerous collections of antique and rare books, a collection of historical Quaker pamphlets, and a large collection of ancient armor and implements of medieval warfare, including seven complete suits of armor, two suits of chainmail, and swords, including an executioner's sword. This collection, from the estate of Colonel T. B. Lawrence, also included "dreadful instruments of torture, hideously suggestive." Perkins measured the losses of the fire in cultural objects, writing, "As we advance in life, we realize that at least one-half of the misfortunes we experience here are the results of our own carelessness or want of knowledge. We were conceited: we thought we knew how to build as well as they do in Europe. We built as we pleased on the account of the negligence of our city authorities. We built poorly, owing to the greed of contractors, and the carelessness of our citizens."

Other observers used other measures. In her book *The Limits of Power*, author Christine Meisner Rosen concluded that the fire spared Boston in other ways.

> *In calculating the fire's impact, it is important to keep in mind that unlike the great Chicago fire, the great Boston fire did not destroy the whole central business district. Quite the contrary, it spared most of the State Street financial district, as well as the wholesale produce and provisions area in the North End and the railroad terminal facilities in the North and South Ends. It also spared the residential sections of the city. All the Boston fire did was devastate the most vital, valuable,*

RUINS OF TRINITY CHURCH, SUMMER STREET.

Trinity Church was damaged beyond repair. From *Harper's Weekly*, November 30, 1872.

part of Boston's business center. . . . The area contained a large number of firms in retail, light manufacturing, publishing, financial and various professional lines of business in addition to almost all the city's boot and shoe, leather, dry good, clothing and textile wholesale activity.

What seems most curious to modern eyes is that there is no verified accurate account of how many people died in the fire. Perkins carefully catalogued the torched torture devices, but there is no one reliable source for the total number of deaths.

The deaths and injuries of firefighters were recorded. Killed were William Farry, foreman of Boston's Ladder Company Number Four; Daniel Cochrane, assistant foreman of Ladder Number Four; and Henry Rogers, a volunteer for Engine Number Six. Farry and Cochrane died when they went to rescue men calling for help in a building and it collapsed, killing all of them. Their bodies were not found for days. Albert D. Abbott and Lewis Porter Abbott, brothers associated with the Charlestown Fire Department, both perished; Lewis died in the collapse of a building on Washington Street, Albert of a broken back days after the fire. Cambridge volunteer fireman William S. Frazier died with Lewis Abbott. Cambridge and Charlestown firemen searched the ruins for bodies for weeks. A surviving Abbott brother was among the searchers when he received word that his mother had collapsed and died from grief and anxiety. The brother left to make funeral arrangements and returned to the search.

Eighteen-year-old Thomas Mahoney, a machinist and volunteer fireman for Worcester, died a few weeks after the fire. According to the *Boston Globe* of November 26, one of his feet was badly smashed and he would not allow the surgeon to amputate it. Infection sealed his fate. Other firefighter deaths were Walter S. Twombly of Malden; Lewis Thompson of Worcester; John Connelly of West Roxbury; and Frank D. Olmstead of Cambridge, who all died in a building on Federal Street. Some reports include firefighter volunteer John Richardson of New Haven, Connecticut, among the dead. He fell from a building while fighting the fire on Sunday morning. Arthur Brayley's fire history, based on the 1872 Boston Fire Department Annual Report, lists him as injured, but other reports indicate he died then or later. Barney O'Neil, the Boston businessman interviewed by the *New York Sun* reporter, said that Connecticut firemen had been transporting a body of a fallen colleague on the train O'Neil rode. Other firemen were severely injured, among them Jacob S. Hook of Malden, William T. Woodward of Dorchester, and A.E. Entell of Worcester. A fund was promptly set up for funeral expenses and to help their families, anchored by $10,000 donated from Hovey's.

The number of other fatalities is difficult to determine. While it was not uncommon at that time to have only estimates of deaths in large fires, it seems odd that the disaster's monetary cost was so carefully calculated when the overall loss of life was not. Various accounts list names of persons killed, but they contain discrepancies. In my book *Boston on Fire*, I estimated that perhaps thirty people, other than firefighters, died in the 1872 fire. Subsequent research indicates that figure might be too high. Brayley's fire history lists Michael Fitzgerald "citizen, Boston" as killed. Two men were buried by a falling building, one or two women died in the Sunday blaze, and there's no record of what happened to the parents of the little lad who asked for help from Damrell or the little girl seen caught in the flames. There were reports, unverified by other sources, of two men caught in wreckage and burned alive as bystanders were unable to help. The body of John Dillon, who had been missing, was identified by the handkerchief in this pocket that bore his name. A reporter for the *New York Sun*, who was at the fire, wrote, "The general opinion is that nearly twenty persons have been either burned to death or were killed by the falling walls. There are rumors that a great many persons are missing, but I can only trace 15 accidents, of which eight are firemen who were injured, and the others are either killed or missing. While so much confusion exists, it is impossible to learn who [is] missing and who the real victims are."

The firefighting community mourned its own. On November 26, Damrell, who was still recovering from damage to his lungs, wrote to the widow of one of the firemen killed in the blaze. In his careful, elegant penmanship, he wrote how much he mourned the loss: The man "rushed with flying footsteps to the succor of those whose voice was heard above the roaring flames and falling walls, crying for help, as it fell on his sensitive ears. While thus engaged in rescuing life, his spirit took its upward flight in company with those he sought to save, using the very element that was carrying destruction over our beloved city."

While the death toll was light compared to Chicago, what Bostonians saw around them in the days after the fire was heartbreaking. "The desolation is bewildering," Reverend Brooks said. The gas had been turned off, so the city was plunged into darkness at night; newspaper editors laid out type by candlelight, kerosene lamps reappeared after years of disuse, and some may have brought out fifty-year-old whale-oil lamps.

Merchants and businessmen visited their former places of operation in the often-vain attempt to salvage anything or set up signs directing customers to their new locations. They often indulged in black humor. "Closed during the hot spell," read a sign hung over a gutted doorway. "We have removed from this location," said another on the sole remaining wall of a tailor's establishment. Another said, "Evicted but not dejected." The *Boston Daily News* reported on November 16 that near the corner of Pearl and High Streets, a white flag had been erected on stake with a sign reading "Fish Market." Hung below that was a twenty-eight-inch eel that had been found stuck in a hose. "It is quite a curiosity," the paper remarked. A merchant who either gave away his stock or had it looted announced that if anyone had ended up with the wrong size footwear, they might come and exchange it for a pair from his new supply. Apparently, many folks who had grabbed merchandise being handed out had second thoughts and returned items to police stations; about $60,000 worth of merchandise was recovered this way. A restaurant reopened under a tent on its former site and reportedly cooked its first dinners on the glowing embers in what had once been its cellar.

The city's papers exhibited their own form of pluck. On November 11, the burned-out *Boston Transcript* published an edition, printed at the plant of the *Boston Globe*, scribe-to-scribe solidarity winning out over rivalry. Under the headline "A Great Calamity," the *Transcript* declared: "Boston which was supposed to possess an immunity against a great conflagration was visited by one beginning on Saturday night, which for the extent and value of property consumed was probably the largest that ever transpired on this continent." The magazine *American Homes* also managed to put out an issue, with only a little delay, and its December edition contained illustrations of the desperate effort to save as much as they could with a nervous horse and exploding buildings. "We lost about eight thousand dollars directly by the fire and full as much more indirectly," the editors wrote. "We hope our friends will urge their friends to subscribe."

Reporters, having spent all their adjectives on the description of the Fire Fiend, now collected oddities: thirteen sailors reported having seen the fire three hundred miles off the coast of Massachusetts; a charred fifty-dollar bill had been picked up in North Abington, twenty-one miles from Boston; the binding of a merchant's ledger was found in East Weymouth, about seventeen miles south; farmers in Portsmouth, New Hampshire, had hurried to help put out a fire they had thought was nearby. The enterprising *Advertiser* published a story—which was widely circulated— on the curious resiliency of paper to fire. For some, however, the fire represented a loss of innocence. In a letter Reverend Brooks wrote: "Run your eye over the map and think what there was between Summer and State and Washington Streets, and consider that all swept away, and it is wretched to think about. . . . The streets that are gone are those that were most familiar to us when we were boys. They were then all residences, and I was born in one, and grew up in another, and went to school in another, and had walked them until I knew all their cobblestones."

The state militia, which had been called out on Sunday, continued to guard the perimeter of the Burnt District. This did not prevent a surge in what we today call "disaster tourism." Bostonians rushed to view the broken streets, and extra trains on the railroads brought thousands of out-of-town gawkers. During the three weeks after the fire, the ruins may have been visited by tens of thousands of people daily. They breathed the sickly smell of smoldering leather and wool and marveled at the wreckage, reminding one observer of the "weird ruins of Stonehenge." Those who could get past the militia cordon gingerly crept through the blasted landscape. "We are in a maze of shadows, where the trickling of water is the only sound that is heard," a reporter wrote.

Burt remained vigilant about mail delivery. On Sunday, even before the fire was stopped, he applied to the city for the use of Faneuil Hall and started moving the mail from the Custom House. He advertised in the

Photographer James W. Black captured the people who thronged to the fire for a glimpse of the disaster. BOSTON PUBLIC LIBRARY

newspaper that the office would be opened as usual at Faneuil Hall on Monday at 10:00 a.m. "This would have been accomplished and everything as we had planned in the morning after but for the fact that the gas was cut off at one o'clock in the morning on account of the second fire and we were obliged to lay in darkness with over one hundred men until daylight losing nearly seven hours," Burt said. All the postal clerks stayed at Faneuil Hall, ate their meals there, and slept on the floor.

A special session of the Massachusetts State Legislature was convened at the request of the Boston City Council, and among its acts was to give authority to the city to make loans to the owners of land in the Burnt District for rebuilding in "sums not to exceed in total $20,000," according to the 1873 Boston City Auditor's Report. Most of Boston's businesses were covered by insurance, but insurance companies likely never anticipated so many claims coming in at once. Twenty of the twenty-nine Massachusetts joint-stock companies doing business at the time would fail due to the large payouts (some companies had liabilities as high as $2.8

million), and some paid out as little as 25 cents on the dollar for losses. Four of the city's fourteen mutual companies were rendered insolvent.

That many businesses retained coverage from major London insurers was dumb luck. Just before the fire, Julius L. Clark, the Massachusetts insurance commissioner, traveled to Liverpool to meet with London insurance companies who covered Boston. The Chicago fire had alarmed the English and they were convinced that the business district in Boston, particularly Franklin and Devonshire Streets, was likely to go up in flames. They told Clark they were preparing to cancel their Boston policies. "I have no doubt that if this fire had not occurred until six months later, instead of about four million and a half which now comes to Boston for the payment of losses from English companies, the risks would have been cancelled to such an extent that probably not more than one-half of that amount would have been found within this burnt district," Clark said.

The news that Boston would likely get coverage of some, if not all, its losses, caused further snark from the Charleston, South Carolina, scribe.

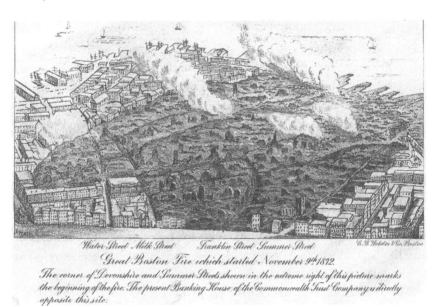

A commercial print card showing the extent of the fire damage. AUTHOR'S COLLECTION

"Thus it will be seen that the 'ruined' merchants will be paid back dollar for dollar for their losses and the ultimate loss will be distributed over a large area, England having a share. No wonder we hear so much about the 'indomitable pluck' of Boston merchants. It is easy enough to be plucky and talking about resuming businesses instantly, when the insurance company stands ready to make you wholesale at once."

However, the city knew many citizens would not be covered by insurance. The day after the fire, a relief committee was formed. A fund of nearly $350,000 was contributed by Boston citizens and placed at the disposal of the relief committee. Hovey's department store pledged $10,000. Mrs. William Claflin, a well-connected Boston matron, launched a committee specifically to help shop girls who had been thrown out of work, saying, "It is a downright blessing to be permitted to see the respectable and brave spirits manifested by these working girls and women." Relief, however, became a kind of political football among the factions of the city government as councilors wrangled over how much money to collect, how much money to give out, and who really deserved assistance. Boston ended up declining some offers of aid and returning nearly $20,000 of relief funds to the donors. The reason? It was feared that "temporary aid might end in permanent support and that the habit of receiving without rendering an equivalent might sap the foundation of that independence of character, and that reliance on one's own resources," Rudnick wrote. "Because of her pride, Boston was to provide for her own victims; because of this prevailing concept of self-reliance, many might have well suffered needlessly during that winter of 1872-1873."

Pundits relentlessly promoted the message: Boston could rebound on its own. The *Boston Advertiser* asserted—perhaps through the pen of Baxter—that "disastrous as the fire has been whatever way we look at it, let no one think of it as irreparable . . . The losers are not turned houseless into the street and there is a sufficiency of necessaries and comforts of life. The loss falls heavily upon trade and investment but economy, good judgement and thrift may recover the losses."

Two of William Lloyd Garrison's sons lost between $3,000 to $10,000 from the inability of insurance to cover their losses. Yet, their father wrote, "Happily the loss fell mainly on that class of our citizens best able to

RESUMING BUSINESS—ON THE SITE OF FRANKLIN'S BIRTH-PLACE.

While it's unlikely that Boston merchants resumed business while the fire was actually burning, many showed extraordinary resilience in opening up stores or offices as soon as they could after the fire. From *Harper's Weekly*, November 30, 1872.

CHANDLER & CO.'S

FULL ACCOUNT OF THE

GREAT FIRE

IN BOSTON!

AND

THE RUINS.

OVER 30 ILLUSTRATIONS.

PUBLISHED BY

W. H. CHANDLER & CO., 21 CORNHILL,

BOSTON, NOVEMBER, 1872.

AT WHOLESALE, ALSO, BY

**NEW ENGLAND NEWS CO., COURT STREET, BOSTON;
AMERICAN NEWS CO., NEW YORK;
WESTERN NEWS CO., CHICAGO.**

Barely ten days after the fire an enterprising publisher produced an account of the disaster, hoping to cash in on interest on the conflagration.

bear it. A number of poor Irish families, at the extreme limits of the conflagration, lost their little all; but the generous contributions that had been made have prevented any sore distress."

Some enterprising folks smelled opportunity. Barely ten days after the fire, the publishers Chandler & Company produced the *Full Account of the Great Fire in Boston! And the Ruins* with more than thirty illustrations. The sixty-one-page account was more florid than factual and it lavished praise on General Burt, saying, "It would have been well had the city been blessed with a few more of the same sort of courageous determined men (like Burt) in the midst of this terrible exigency—although, unquestionably, everyone in authority did 'his level best' in this trying hour." On the back page of this booklet, Morris & Ireland Safes

Safe manufacturers saw a chance to hawk their products with advertisements about their fire-resistant models. From Chandler's *Full Account of the Great Fire in Boston.*

took out a full-page advertisement to highlight glowing testimonials of their products' indestructibility. Said one: "Gentlemen: We this morning opened our safe and found our books, money and papers preserved intact, nothing but the binding of the books being scorched."

CHAPTER 12

Who Is to Blame?

This danger had been foreseen and our calamity had been foretold both here and abroad.

—REPORT OF THE COMMISSIONERS APPOINTED
TO INVESTIGATE THE CAUSE AND MANAGEMENT
OF THE GREAT FIRE IN BOSTON

CHIEF ENGINEER JOHN DAMRELL CHOSE HIS WORDS CAREFULLY. "I HAVE thought the matter over; have gone over the ground—and have fought it over in my mind, again and again, and I say, candidly, that I know of no place where I could change my tactics, in any way, shape, or manner, with the exception of the use of gunpowder, and that I would not do. If I were to fight that over again in other sections, I probably should use gunpowder under other circumstances, but in this district, I would not change my tactics."

On December 3, three weeks after the fire, Damrell was on the witness stand to testify before an unusual commission, one tasked with determining why the city of Boston had nearly burned down. Just four days after the fire, Mayor Gaston appointed a "scientific commission" to "investigate the cause of the recent fire and the efforts made for its suppression." Whatever one might think about the conclusions in the *Report of the Commissioners Appointed to Investigate the Cause and Management of the Great Fire In Boston*," one has to admire the unnamed stenographer(s) who recorded the hours and hours of testimony, seemingly verbatim, that provides us with a clear and compelling record of the actors in the drama of November 9 to 11.

The prominent men involved in the testimony about the Great Boston Fire: Mayor Gaston, Chief Damrell, and Police Chief Savage. From Arthur Brayley's *A Complete History of the Boston Fire Department*.

Much of what we know of this fire is contained in the testimony of the about two hundred witnesses heard in forty-two sessions, beginning November 26, 1872. While Damrell was clearly the main focus—he testified four times—the parade of witnesses ranged from onlookers to firemen to city officials to "everyone whose name was suggested." Their words seem to have been recorded verbatim. The five commissioners, their names listed as Thomas Russell, Charles G. Greene, Samuel C. Cobb, A. Firth, and E.S. Philbrick, were drawn from the ranks of Boston's leaders.

The testimony ranged "from the laconic statements of practical firemen, jealous of the honor of the service, to the wild declarations of excitable persons who dreamed dreams and saw visions," as Harold Murdock commented. As is often the case with testimony, the witnesses frequently contradicted each other on facts and indulged in opinion and speculation. Augustine Sanderson, Clarence Dorr, and Officer John Page testified about the start of the fire. Engineer Jacobs, foreman Marden, and other firemen spoke of how the blaze was fought and managed. Alderman Woolley recounted in clear detail his clash with General Benham. Also called in was Mansard gadfly Joseph Bird, reveling in the attention to his previous complaints. Harvard President Charles Eliot described how he had given advice to Damrell about placement of hoses "but it was not done." Alderman Flanders recounted Damrell's clashes with the water board and described its cavalier attitude about removing hydrants without informing the fire department. Prominent architect Nathaniel Bradlee, a member and a former president of the Boston Water Board, gave sullen and short answers that directly contradicted Damrell's testimony. He said the downtown's water mains were not calculated for conflagrations and enlarging them would not be worth the expense. As for Lowry hydrants, he said, "I don't see that there is any advantage over the other hydrants, although firemen claim that they are." The commissioners ultimately dismissed much of the testimony as immaterial, irrelevant, and hearsay.

The commissioners wanted to know why the fire department didn't bring in more horses. One fireman tried to explain that doing so wasn't easy: "We went to one or two places with a view to get horses, but we found they were in as bad condition as our own. As to taking green horses, that is one of the worst things in the world. If you harness green horses to an engine, they are sensitive to the flying cinders, the smoke, and the shouting in the streets, and it is not easy to control them. For instance, we have driven the horses up to a building on fire and found that it was impossible to drive them through the smoke." The man recounted an incident in Cambridge where the company was hemmed in by a fire: "An ordinary pair of horses would never have brought the engine out, but our trained horses came right through the flames."

In a line of questioning that was especially galling to Damrell, commissioners asked nearly everyone who had an interaction

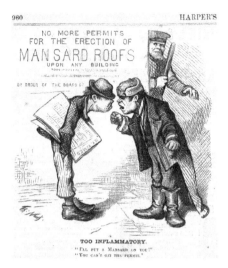

Famed cartoonist Thomas Nast creates his own spin on attitudes about Mansard roofs in the December 7, 1872, issue of *Harper's Weekly*.

with the chief about his mental state, influenced by reports that he was emotionally out of control. Eliot said, for example, when he was looking for Damrell that firemen told him he had gone to the Insane Hospital, and another said he had lost his head. Others recounted a clash between Damrell and a building owner who insisted his property be saved. But most of those who had dealings with Damrell said he was calm and focused. "I saw nothing unusual with him," fireman John Colligan said, in a typical response. "He discussed matters as he always does, in his quick way, but there was no excitement about him at all." Many, however, passed judgment indirectly on Damrell. "I felt then, and I feel today, more sorrow over the bad management of the fire, as it seems to me—that is to say, the disgrace of it—than over the loss," Eliot sniffed.

Curiously, there is nothing in the report or testimony indicating that the deaths of the eleven firemen and volunteers should be investigated. The commissioners did lavish praise on the men in their final report. "No battle-field ever witnessed nobler heroism than was seen in our streets."

But aside from an acknowledgment that "More than one of our firemen has literally proved 'faithful unto death,'" the commissioners did not seem overly curious as to how these heroes fell and what, if anything, could be done to prevent future deaths.

When the commissioners were not focusing on Damrell's mental state, they were hammering away with questions about the use of gunpowder. Was it effective? Did it spread the fire? Or did it save the city? Those who had their buildings blown up were threatening legal action, Burt's nonchalant dismissal of the law notwithstanding, and the commissioners wanted to determine if exploding buildings had been a wise choice. Damrell said no, that the explosions spread the fire, and he deeply regretted his actions that gave citizens permission to blow up buildings. Gunpowder might be useful in some circumstances, but not in this fire.

General Burt staunchly defended the use of gunpowder. He faulted the escaping gas for spreading flames. "The gas of this city is a more serious danger to life and property than any convenient thing we have. In my judgment, we could have stayed the fire long before we did but for the gas," he said. But he lavished praise on firefighters and came to Damrell's defense by backing up the chief's contentions about water supply and inadequate apparatus, declaring in his take-no-prisoner style, "The Fire Department of this city, in its engines, is entirely inadequate to our wants. We ought to have to-day two steam fire engines of not less than ten tons, requiring from four to six horses, capable of throwing a three or four-inch stream, through a wire-bound hose, two hundred feet in height. The Fire Department of this city today is just as incompetent to cope with the fires we are liable to have, as it was fifteen years ago, when we outgrew the hand engines."

Ever the politician, Gaston relied on that old standby: *I don't recall.* Asked if he gave General Burt authority to blow up buildings, he replied, "I have no recollection of giving him any such authority. I understood the authority to proceed from the Chief Engineer. There were a great number of things said that night. Of course, I don't remember everything that was said; but my purpose was to let the responsibility rest where the law placed it, and so far, as I can recollect, I endeavored to act consistently with that purpose. My impression is that the authority came in writing from the Chief Engineer to Gen. Burt. I did not intend to give Gen. Burt any authority; I did not have it to give."

By contrast, Damrell remembered the events with great clarity. "If my memory serves me right, I listened to some remarks from Mr. Burt, who went on to say that he wanted the gates of the Common opened that goods might be carried there. He wanted the militia turned out and wanted somebody sent to the Navy Yard to get powder. He wanted the Mayor or Chief Engineer, to organize parties of gentlemen, composed of one hundred citizens, who should have authority to remove goods and to blow up buildings. I think that was the extent of the work that he wished done. I notified him that I was ready to receive the assistance of any gentlemen, and would authorize them to remove goods, or to do such other work as the exigency of the case might demand, even to the blowing up of buildings, and as the Board of Engineers had authorized me to blow up buildings, I cheerfully would receive any aid that they might offer in that direction. I believe that is about all. I then sat down at the table and wrote that A, B, and C, or the gentlemen who were there—Mr. Burt, I think, was one; Gen. Benham was another; the Hon. George O. Carpenter another; Colonel Shepard another; Alderman Jenks another; Mr. Allen, President of the Water Board, another; and L. Foster Morse, another."

Such details do not indicate Damrell was trying to avoid responsibility; rather, he hoped to buttress his stance as a leader who would listen to reasonable suggestions. As someone who never finished high school, Damrell was facing men of distinction, such as the Harvard-educated lawyer Burt. He did not blame the use of gunpowder on these men as much as he blamed himself for giving them the authority. "I confess to a weakness of which I am ashamed, that pressured as I was, I gave authority to certain men to do certain work without [putting them under] my command, or my engineers," he testified. He "felt that the experiment must be tried, or the citizens would never feel satisfied if it was not done." Still, he regretted his actions.

On the last day of the hearings on January 11, 1873, General Henry W. Benham testified; he was questioned primarily about the use of gunpowder. He described the buildings he had ordered blown up, explaining

General Henry W. Benham. LIBRARY OF CONGRESS

he chose them carefully, although he did not always remain to witness the explosions.

"Did you at any time send a message to Mr. Damrell that you would 'blow up State Street, Damrell or no Damrell,' or any words to that effect?" he was asked.

"No, sir. I never heard such words used by anyone before." Benham insisted he had been courteous to Damrell, whose manner "appeared somewhat excited or irritated," and he believed that Damrell had given permission to use gunpowder. Benham's account of his encounter with Alderman Woolley was brief and free of rancorous details; Woolley was "earnest but not offensive to me," he said.

Benham saved his harshest words for the fire management. "If a general has not a fixed position on the battlefield, he is of very little use. I look upon the position of the chief engineer as similar to that, and instead of being in the fire, or doing a private's duty as I might say, or a fireman's duty, I think it is of the first importance that he should have a place where every foreman of an engine, and every magistrate or other person could know where to go to consult him. If the fire was near the City Hall, he might have his headquarters there. He might, of course, occasionally make a personal reconnaissance, but in that case, he should have a person in his position to inform those who came for consultation or directions. On the march I always had a fixed position, about one-third of the way from the head of the column usually."

The hearings concluded with brief comments from a meek clerk from Mayor Gaston's office. "I was there all the time with the Mayor and heard him give no one authority to blow up buildings," said James R. Carret. "General Benham repeated his request and urged that he might receive authority from the mayor but was repeatedly refused."

At the end of January 1873, the commission issued its findings.

The question of the fire's cause was summarily dealt with in the first pages of the final report. The commissioners concluded the fire clearly began in or near the elevator of the Tebbetts building at 83-85 Summer Street, likely in the basement ceiling at the rear of the building. "To the more important question of how the fire began no answer can be given." There was no evidence of arson. The more important questions were why did the fire spread so quickly and roar out of control, and was it managed effectively?

The commission blamed the quick spread of the fire on the delays in getting fire companies early to the fire. The report acknowledged that the difference in speed between horse and foot power was less than the general public supposed, yet "time was invaluable and time was lost." The commission concluded that horses should have been commandeered and quickly trained.

Damrell would insist that commandeering horses was, indeed, part of his orders, but there were simply none to be had. It was a sensitive issue on another front. Some newspapers complained that the horses had been babied at the expense of the city's safety. The animal welfare newsletter, *Our Dumb Animals*, had to write a short story defending its actions in protecting the sick horses, saying that, "In an emergency like that of Saturday night, no action of ours would have prevented the use of the department horses, even at the sacrifice of their lives."

The commission did agree with Damrell on some key points—they singled out the danger of the buildings' heights and general faulty construction. "The insufficient supply of water was felt at the outset, and was, without doubt, one cause of the conflagration." They noted the city might need more fire alarm boxes and a better system for unlocking them. "The annoyance of an occasional false alarm is not to be weighed against the dangers of delay."

As for the use of gunpowder, the commissioner was unsure if it had helped or hurt. However, all agreed that "explosives never should be used again as they were at that time, and that, if used at all, we should be prepared to employ them skillfully, carefully, and by a fixed plan." It was an error, as Damrell acknowledged, to give citizens the authority to blow up buildings. The commissioner upped the ante by suggesting another option. "Dynamite, sometimes known as 'Giant Powder,' is ten times as powerful as gunpowder and can bring down a building, rather than to scatter its materials."

As for Damrell, "he deserved all praise for his courage, he shrank from no exertion and from no danger," the commission found. He was cool and focused. However, the commissioners—in what can only be a play to shift any responsibility from the city's government and infrastructure—said Damrell should have been better prepared for a terrible fire. The very fact that he knew the area was dangerous meant he should have been ready. The response was piecemeal and "the heroism of individuals was too often wasted, because it was not directed by a master-mind."

This was the chief complaint—that Damrell acted more as a soldier than a general. "The Chief seems to have performed the duties of a fireman from time to time, now placing a ladder, now performing some act of humanity, now applying fire to a mine. In a word, he tried to unite the services of a private with those of a commander-in-chief. It seems to us that, at such a time, the Head of the Force should remain for the most part in some accessible place where he could command a view of the conflagration—a place known to his subordinates, where he could receive reports from them, and send them his orders." This may have reflected the way the social classes view labor—the Brahmin general must retain superiority over the working-class foot soldiers.

Thus, when Damrell politely rebuffed General Benham's suggestion that he remain at City Hall, Damrell was not behaving as a military commander should. While Damrell was never the type to stand back and let others do the work for him, could he be faulted for not having an overall plan of attack? Many believe that once the fire spread well across Summer Street and into Winthrop Square, there appears to have been no definite concerted plan to stop it.

In effect, the commission's report held Damrell largely responsible (and Mayor Gaston to a lesser degree). In the months after the fire, Damrell was viewed by many in the city—particularly businessmen whose buildings were blown up—as the man who let Boston burn. Burt, by contrast, was heralded as a man of action.

Damrell bore the criticism stoically. He drew deep satisfaction from a letter of support from firemen that said "the ability, coolness, indomitable courage and perseverance displayed by Chief Engineer John S. Damrell, in his efforts to arrest the progress of the fire, merits, and receives, our earnest and unqualified approbation." He never wavered from his belief that he belonged at the front lines and that he trusted his engineers to fight the fire based on their experience, their familiarity with the district, its water supply, and its buildings.

In a show of support, he was re-elected chief in April 1873. Shortly before that, in January 1873, a fifty-five-ton fire boat, its hull made of iron, was put into service. Its Amoskeag-built fire engines could play eight streams at one time and was equal in capacity to four first-class fire engines. The cost was $19,893.95. It was christened the William M. Flanders, after the city councilor who had been head of the fire committee, and who spoke in detail during the commissioner's investigation about clashes with the city's Water Board. Damrell's 1872 Annual Report spoke proudly of the new addition. "The experience of the past years has shown conclusively that this boat will prove a valuable and effective auxiliary to our Fire Department, commanding as it does a larger field of operation than any four steam fire engines in commission."

Damrell knew that Boston was not unique, nor was Chicago an aberration. Huge conflagrations happened with alarming frequency in the latter half of the nineteenth and early twentieth centuries. In August 1873, a major fire destroyed the downtown of Portland, Oregon. Fires would also devastate Baltimore and San Francisco. Damrell began to think in national terms. He had learned much from the firemen in Chicago and from General Sheridan on the use of gunpowder, and about Lowry hydrants from the Salem Massachusetts Fire Department. A national organization of fire chiefs could allow for exchange of information on the latest equipment and techniques. He began to reach out to other chiefs, and, in the fall of 1873, he became founder and first president of the National Association of Fire Engineers. This organization later became the International Association of Fire Chiefs, which today describes its members as "the world's leading experts in firefighting, emergency medical services, terrorism response, hazardous materials spills, natural disasters, search and rescue, and public safety policy."

Even so, political forces in Boston were moving in ways that would force Damrell to leave the profession he so loved. Boston's city leaders decided the fire department needed even more oversight, particularly after another bad fire on Washington Street near Boylston Street in a five-story furniture warehouse on May 30, 1873. The so-called Memorial Day Fire spread over four acres, destroyed thirty buildings, including a pianoforte warehouse and Boston's elegant Globe Theatre, billed as "the Parlor of Comedy." From $1 million to $2 million in damage was caused. About ten of the parties burnt out in May were also burnt out in the November Great Fire, according to city documents, where an unnamed bureaucrat wrote, "This has added, in a short space of a little over six months, another burden for our people to bear and struck a blow at our prosperity." The *Boston Globe's* May 31 headline lamented, "Another Great Fire."

In response, a citizens' petition was filed with the city council pushing for an independent board to have control and management over the fire department. The proposal was fiercely debated. Proponents argued that the new paid commission would lead to a system of "military discipline and responsibility, together with such instruction, training, and drill, theoretical as well as practical, as shall bring it to the highest state of efficiency." The opposition contended the board of engineers already acted as a kind of commission and did all the work, that it would be expensive and that commissioners who would have control over the livelihood of five hundred employees—and thus five hundred voters— "would be a political force, capable of controlling almost any municipal election." Charles Taylor, the author of the 1972 *Globe* anniversary supplement on the Great Fire, would recognize the old-style politics at play.

The proponents won. The new system was adopted in October 1873, less than a year after the Great Fire; three commissioners were appointed by the mayor, approved by the council, and assumed their duties on November 20. They now oversaw the chief engineer, the assistant chiefs (who were made permanent employees instead of being elected), the fire-alarm superintendent, and other officers and firemen. The number of assistant chiefs was reduced from fourteen to ten; the *Boston Globe* reported that many of those would likely resign, as their businesses were likely more profitable than full-time fire duty.

Damrell had had enough. He announced he would resign as chief; he was succeeded in April 1874 by assistant engineer William Green.

That might have been the last chapter in Damrell's story as a public servant. He could have returned to his profitable building business, renamed J. Damrell & Son when his oldest son joined him. He might have been content to leave the byzantine world of Boston politics behind.

That did not happen.

CHAPTER 13

Rebuilt and Reborn

In two years, all signs of the conflagration had disappeared and in a slightly longer period, the ministers of the town and its leading after-dinner speakers had even wearied of the once compelling phrase "springing Phoenix-like from the ashes." The Great Fire was a thing of the past.

—Lucius Beebe
Boston and the Boston Legend

Given what Boston's literati had seen, you might think more than a few of them would have written more than letters about the fire. Oliver Wendell Holmes Sr., at least, wrote one of his stirring poems, titled "After the Fire." In the novel *Virgil Drops His Cane*, Frank Pratt pens a sentimental story of fatherly love that weaves in many of the fire's legends. *Little Women* author Louisa May Alcott was also inspired.

Alcott referred only briefly to the fire in extant letters or diaries, once describing herself, in reference to her acting: "When I don't look like the tragic muse, I look like the ghostly relic of the great Boston fire." She could not get the thought of that lone spotted dog out of her head. In a short story called "Huckleberry," published in the *Youth Companion* in January 1873, a narrator describes walking through the ruins of a great fire and seeing a spotted dog lying on the edge of a smoking cellar. "Faithful fellow! He is still watching his master's property, I dare say, though everything is in ashes." The narrator brings the poor beast to her abode and finds him a home before he dies a sad, but sentimental, death at his mistress's feet. It was not Alcott at her finest, but her story is one of the

A photo from circa 1900 of the grand US Post Office and Sub Treasury Building. This building was torn down in 1929.

few places the Great Fire crept into literature, albeit in this case a pulp magazine for boys.

As the disaster tourists dispersed, as photographers Soule and Black reaped rewards from their labors, the work of rebuilding went on. Rubble was cleared away—some of it used for landfill to add to South Boston—damaged buildings torn down, and plans made for rebuilding. The new Post Office building had survived, to General Burt's great satisfaction. He relocated mail operations to Faneuil Hall in the meantime, proudly declaring that not one letter was lost. Nearby, rubble was cleared and Post Office Square was established. Reverend Brooks said goodbye to the old Trinity Church and turned his attention to the new one, the imposing structure designed by famed architect Henry Hobson Richardson, underway at Copley Square. Completed in 1877, it still stands today, near the finish line of the Boston Marathon. On November 16, the *Advertiser* cheerfully reported, "The appearance of the 'burnt district' was considerably changed yesterday by the operation of the gangs of workmen employed in tearing down and cleaning away. The debris is nearly entirely cleared out of High and Purchase Streets. Milk Street is clear, part of Franklin Street is open, the passages along the harbor front are free."

Where some saw ruin, others saw opportunity, among them General Burt. "It seems to me, we should have, here in Boston, with the opening and opportunity that the Burnt District gives us, a new and distinct plan for protection against fires made to conform to the wants of the city for business purposes. We need it for health, we need it for convenience in our business," he testified before the commissioners investigating the fire.

On November 10, 1873, a group of city officials marked the first anniversary of the fire with a solemn event. A party of dignitaries toured the streets of the Burnt District. Some 365 iron, brick, and stone buildings were under construction, and 115 were nearly completed. They now had external walls of twenty inches thick to a height of two stories and sixteen inches thick above that. The exterior finish of the roof was noncombustible, with galvanized iron used for cornices and other projections, according to the *Boston Globe*.

A note of self-satisfaction crept into the *Globe*'s coverage. "It is hard to realize that a year ago Boston was experiencing the ravages of a fearful conflagration which laid in ash the finest business quarter of the city. No one who witnessed the scenes of that terrible fire would have believed that in a year from the time of its occurrence the greater part of the territory which it ravaged would be covered with buildings superior in solidity as well as in architectural elegance and beauty to those that were then destroyed." Past errors, however, had to be "burnt into" us.

Immediately after the fire, there was much discussion of taking the opportunity to rearrange the lines of the city's streets and get rid of the crooked "cow-path" layout. Rosen noted that Burt was among those pushing for a series of improvements over a lengthy period of time to create fire barriers in the commercial area and make the Burnt District the center of a new city-wide traffic system. Burt's plan was even published in the *Boston Advertiser*, although apparently the *Advertiser*, reflecting the view of the business community, took a dim view of radical improvements. On

The following is a diagram of the proposed revision of streets in the burnt district, prepared at the City Hall under the general direction of the committee on streets.

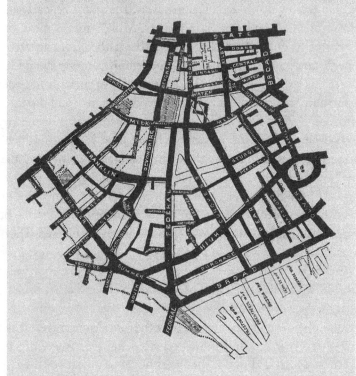

On this plan the black lines stand for the existing streets; the irregular dotted line, from near Liverpool Wharf to Congress Square and thence, through Washington and Summer, to Federal Street, marks the boundary of the fire. The light lines in the drawing indicate the proposed widenings and extensions. The principal changes are these: Federal Street is made a main avenue, eighty feet wide, to the foot of Summer Street, and so on to South Boston; widened on the right coming toward State Street, and swinging to the right from the foot of Franklin Street, so as to pass the new post office on the east side into Congress Street, which is widened on the left to State.

Summer Street is widened on the left, going from Washington in several places, and on the right between Lincoln and South streets.

Washington Street is widened to sixty feet on the right coming toward Cornhill.

Bedford Street is widened on the right going from Kingston to Church Green, and the Church Green lot is rounded off.

Franklin Street is extended across Devonshire, Federal, and Congress streets to Sturgis, and is widened on the south side between Devonshire and Federal.

Hawley Street is widened to forty feet, mainly on the right from Summer, and is cut through to Milk Street.

Chauncy Street is widened and cut through to the junction of Devonshire and Milk streets; and Arch Street is discontinued.

Otis Street is widened on the right from Summer to Winthrop Square, and on the left to Franklin Street.

Devonshire Street is widened on the left from Summer to Winthrop Square, and straightened and widened on the right to Milk.

Congress Street is widened on the right from Broad to the junction with Federal Street, and thence discontinued.

Pearl Street is carried to the junction of Water and Federal streets.

Milk Street is widened on the right from Washington to Broad Street; and Water Street on the left to Batterymarch.

Broad Street is widened on the water side from Summer to Oliver; and Purchase is widened on the right from Summer Street.

[135]

In his book on the fire, Harold Murdock reprints one of the many maps printed in local newspapers about proposed street changes in Boston. Most of these changes did not come to pass.

November 16, the *Boston Post* said this opportunity should not be wasted. "What was an irregular assemblance of narrow and sinuous streets may thus become the finest portion of the city, with broad highways and solid and fire-defying structure."

Alas for those of us who often get mired in the wicked twists and turns of the downtown street. Pity the poor tourist who likely wonders how to ever escape the repeating temporal loops of one-way streets! The villain of Taylor's *Boston Globe* supplement—what he dubbed old-fashioned politics—made yet another appearance. "The people of Boston quickly discovered that [the fire] has not altered the many powerful political, technological, and economic factors that had always stood in the way of optimal redevelopment," writes Christine Meisner Rosen in *The Limits of Power: Great Fires and the Process of City Growth in America*.

The city did purchase land to widen and extend some downtown streets. Franklin Street, which had extended only to Federal Street, was cut through to Pearl Street, there to meet what had been Sturgis Street. Landowners' opposition, however, prevented the city from making more substantial changes. Different factions clashed over the use of eminent domain and the cost to taxpayers of taking so much land—citizens may have wanted change, but they didn't want to pay for it. Burt invested his considerable energy and Washington, DC, connections and clout to push for a widening of Water Street and the creation of Post Office Square near the new Post Office building despite considerable opposition from the City Council. Burt won the day on the Post Office Square issue but lost the battle for other improvements in what Rosen characterized as "cut-throat competition" among landowners and politicians.

"As a result, the community consensus concerning the desirability of improvement disintegrated, and the opportunity to achieve many greatly needed individual improvements soon slipped beyond the city's grasp," Rosen wrote. Rudnick put this another way: "It is thus not too harsh a judgment to state that [Boston's] plans for the reconstruction of the 'Burnt District' constituted a tragic failure." Rudnick and Rosen reached a similar conclusion: Boston could have turned the disaster into an opportunity to remake and enhance the city.

THE REBUILDING OF PEARL STREET : MAY, 1873.

Boston moved quickly to rebuild as this illustration of Pearl Street in May 1873 in the *Boston Illustrated* pamphlet indicates.

What Boston really wanted to do was to move on quickly. The fire had—paradoxically enough—made land more valuable in the downtown. Shortly after the fire, land on Summer Street opposite Church Green, then assessed for $11 per square foot, sold for $17 a square foot. Professors Richard Hornbeck of the University of Chicago and Daniel Keniston of Louisiana State University analyzed city tax-assessment data and supplemental data about plots in the Burnt District and surrounding areas in 1867, 1869, 1871, 1872, 1873, 1882, and 1894. Rather than being a drag on the city's fortunes, the Fire Fiend actually boosted them. "We estimate that the Fire generated substantial economic gains, capitalized in higher land values. Land values increased substantially in the burned area, and by a similar magnitude in nearby unburned areas," the two economists wrote in their fittingly titled 2017 *American Economic Review* article "Creative Destruction: Barriers to Urban Growth and the Great Boston Fire of 1872."

Still there was a groundswell of support for change in safety issues and a reaction against the city's water board. Based on Boston City Auditor records, Rosen concludes,

> *Badly embarrassed by their own and the Water Board's negligence, the members of the City Council took matters into their own hand by appropriating $85,000 of city funds to force the [water board] to make . . . improvements. As a result, the Board, equally embarrassed, finally began replacing the old six-inch mains and the two- to four-inch rust-encrusted distribution pipes [to hydrants] with new eight- and twelve-inch mains and new coal-tar covered feeder pipes. It also began replacing antiquated hydrants with large new Lowry hydrants. By the spring of 1874, it had repiped almost every street in the Burnt District and had replaced eighty-three of the old hydrants with 113 Lowry hydrants which it laid at distances never exceeding 260 feet.*

The fire also pushed the Water Board to make improvements in the rest of the city and the destructive Memorial Day fire of 1873 led to more fire-prevention improvements. Still there was a reluctance to further loosen purse strings. The Water Board declined to meet all of Damrell's requests, considering them "too liberal" and continued to ignore the City Council's repeated demands for additional safety improvements. "The Great Fire caused enough of a public outcry to force the Water Board to correct its most ruinous failures but it did not produce a shock sufficient to force the board to adopt new goals," Rosen writes. Given the destruction around it, one wonders what kind of a shock was required to force the Water Board to be more aggressive in its innovations.

In a few years, nearly all traces of the Burnt District had disappeared. Some businesspeople struggled for years, including Seman Klous, who owned the building where the fire originated. In 1992, his granddaughter Margaret W. Williams wrote an account of the fire for the *New Hampshire Union Leader* newspaper. "Not only did Grandpa never completely recover financially from the fire, he also never ceased to regret that it had started in a Klous Building, thus bringing disaster not only to him, but to many others," she wrote.

Hovey's Department Store remained in business for decades. William Endicott, Jr., who had become a partner in 1851, retired in 1910 after sixty-four years. In 1947, Jordan Marsh, then one of Boston's most enduring retail outlets, took over Hovey's business, literally breaking down the walls between the two enterprises.

Patrick Donahoe, who watched as the *Pilot* building burned, regrouped only to see the newspaper burnt out again in another building just ten days later, causing him to remark with grim humor that he was "tired of Phoenixing." He declared bankruptcy in 1876. John Joseph Williams, the first Archbishop of the Archdiocese of Boston, purchased the *Pilot* to help out. Donahoe then started *Donahoe's Magazine*, a Catholic and Irish American monthly, and in 1881, he was able to buy back the *Pilot* and devoted his remaining years to its management. He died in Boston on March 18, 1901, one day after his ninetieth birthday.

Nathaniel Bradlee, a member and president of the Boston Water Board—that body that so bedeviled Damrell—made a killing from the Great Fire. The well-known architect worked on about sixty projects in the ensuing two years, many of which involved reconstructing buildings he had first designed in the 1850s and 1860s. He also ran unsuccessfully for mayor in 1876.

Burt, like Damrell and Gaston, was named in various suits related to the blowing up of buildings during the fire, but that did not seem to affect him. In early 1876, after nine years, Burt left his position as postmaster. At a farewell dinner reported by the *Globe* on January 3, 1876, he spoke of his efforts to make Post Office Square "the most beautiful locality in the city of Boston, wrought out and built up among the wreck and ruin of the mighty fire." He returned to work as an attorney in the railroad business and died in 1882 at age fifty-two in Sarasota, New York. He was buried in Mount Auburn Cemetery.

The calamity had an unusual effect on reporter Sylvester Baxter. It triggered an interest in city planning and green spaces. Certainly, as a reporter for the *Advertiser* until 1875, he had a front-row seat to fierce debates about how to rebuild after the fire. In 1875, Baxter took off for Germany, where he studied at the universities of Leipzig and Berlin and served as the *Advertiser's* correspondent in Europe. In 1881 he joined an archeological expedition to investigate Zuni ruins in the American Southwest, and in 1882, he wrote about the visit of several Zuni chiefs to Washington and Boston, where the Zuni conducted a sunrise ceremony on the beach at Deer Island, which had been used as a kind of concentration camp for Native Americans during King Philip's War (or Metacom's Rebellion) in the 1670s.

Sylvester Baxter in 1893

He began working for the *Boston Herald* in 1880, where he wrote articles promoting the expansion of the city's municipal park system, including lobbying for the preservation of the Middlesex Fells, a beautiful tract of undeveloped land north of Boston (which begins just blocks from my house.) Baxter teamed up with Charles Eliot, a son of the Harvard president, who had apprenticed with Frederick Law Olmsted during the time the famed landscape architect envisioned Boston's "Emerald Necklace" of parks. Baxter and Eliot had a vision of a "greater Boston," a kind of "Emerald Metropolis." Largely through their efforts, the Metropolitan Park Commission, the nation's first regional park system, was authorized in 1893. The new commission acquired more than nine thousand acres in six years, according to Karl Haglund, who wrote about the development of the park system in Nancy S. Seasholes's *The Atlas of Boston History*. This was a gift for many future generations of Bostonians.

Baxter later settled in Malden, a city just outside Boston, and wrote books on European city planning and Spanish Colonial architecture in

Mexico, as well as travel books on New England. He died in 1927 in San Juan, Puerto Rico. Sylvester Baxter Riverfront Park in Somerville is named for him. The man who had burned his shoes covering the Great Boston Fire used that experience to push for more green and open spaces within an urban area.

For decades, Bostonians continued to mark the anniversary of the fire. Papers put special editions on the tenth, twentieth, fiftieth, and, finally, the one-hundredth anniversaries. A fire buff group, the Box 52 Association, was formed in 1912. Prolific Boston historian and author Anthony Mitchell Sammarco produced a 1997 book, *The Great Boston Fire of 1872*, which pulled together many of the most striking photographs of the aftermath of the conflagration. Bruce Twickler produced a documentary that used emerging digital technology to create a virtual Boston of 1872 and virtually burn it down. But for the most part—unlike the Chicago Fire—the Great Boston Fire began to recede from the public imagination.

For one man, the memory never faded.

CHAPTER 14

Damrell's Last Stand

John S. Damrell could never stray far from the front lines. When he left the fire service in 1874, he returned to his building business, but he was also beset by lawsuits relating to the destruction of buildings during the Great Fire of 1872. He had many other interests: He was a devoted Sunday School teacher and he served as a trustee of the Massachusetts School for the Feeble-Minded (as institutions like that were called in those days). He was a member of numerous social clubs and men's organizations. But ever the fighter, he returned to public service.

In November 1877, Damrell was appointed Inspector of Buildings for the city of Boston, a job also known as Building Commissioner. His son Charles became his clerk and right-hand man. For the next twenty-five years, into the dawn of the twentieth century, Damrell attempted to ensure that Boston's buildings would comply with increasingly strict building codes to make the city safer. Soon after his appointment, he brought together builders, architects, and owners to consider amendments to the building laws and regulations for building construction. He continued to be a gadfly, constantly pushing for stricter building codes in his reports to the city council.

Damrell also continued his national advocacy. In 1891 he founded and was elected the first president of the National Association of Commissioners and Inspectors of Public Buildings (NACIPB). That year, he joined underwriters, architects, builders, building inspectors, and fire chiefs in supporting "general suggestions" for stricter guidelines for building construction to improve fire resistance and fire safety laws to be recommended to all state legislatures. This step set the stage for 1905, when

This unusual cartoon from the *Boston Journal of Commerce* from 1873 lampoons grandiose plans to memorialize the Great Boston Fire. Many figures of the day can be seen in here, including Damrell, and atop the monument, architect Nathaniel Jeremiah Bradlee. Obviously, not everyone considered Boston's survival a triumph. COURTESY OF *BOSTON ATHENAEUM*

the National Board of Fire Underwriters published the first edition of its *Recommended Building Code,* later the *National Building Code* (NBC), a landmark document that provides guidelines for residential, commercial, institutional, and educational construction. Bruce Twickler, who turned his 2006 documentary on the 1872 fire into an homage to Damrell, believes the move to a national building code is why he concluded Damrell was the firefighter who saved American cities from burning down.

If living well can be considered the best revenge, Damrell surely dined on that dish best served cold. Judging by the frequent mentions of his name in the *Boston Globe,* he enjoyed status as an honored member of the city's political and business elite. Often called upon to give speeches at events and funerals, his opinions were respectfully cited about fire and safety issues. He gained national stature as a fire safety visionary for his work with the National Association of Fire Engineers. On August 6, 1888, the fire-service newspaper the *Baltimore Underwriter* declared his selection as the organization's president a "peculiarly happy one," both an endorsement of his actions during the Great Fire and a protest against "the censure so freely bestowed upon him for faults over which he had not the least measure of control and for which he was no more responsible than the humblest citizen."

In 1883, while vacationing on Martha's Vineyard, Damrell was called into action when a large fire broke out in Vineyard Haven. He "was gladly hailed by owners of threatened buildings" and given control by the town authorities. "Under his direction and good judgment, a wise selection was made of places to stand and fight the burning element," reported the *Evening Standard*.

In 1886, he bought property and moved next to Charles's house in the bucolic town of Dover, west of Boston. He retired as Boston's building inspector in 1903, after the election of Mayor Patrick Andrew Collins, and was succeeded by his son Charles, who later wrote a massive book about Boston's building history.

In his final *Annual Report for the Building Department*, submitted in February 1903, Damrell included records for gas and elevator accidents complete with victims' names and the circumstances and causes of their injuries or deaths. "It is clear that preventable deaths continued to haunt him and that he habitually gathered data related to safety issues that could be addressed by improvements in procedures or amendments to codes," said Twickler.

The mental anguish caused by the fire persisted for years. On February 2, 1886, Damrell gave a lengthy speech in a meeting for the Boston Veteran Firemen, speaking candidly of the fire's searing aftermath and the disdain that businessmen who lost money in the fire felt for him.

"I have no doubt many believe that the Chief Engineer was the city's Jonah and he was either drunk or crazy or both and had suddenly lost his senses," he said, the sting of all those questions about his sanity undoubtedly still pricking him. "If I could have been proved unstrung by excitement, and not capable of issuing proper orders, or had lost the confidence of my intelligent Board of Engineers, the ignorance and want of common sense—as apparent in their methods of doing business—would be transferred to my shoulders."

He looked out at his audience, which included men he had worked with for years and men he knew were willing to sacrifice themselves for others, even for those who would top their buildings with ostentatious Mansard roofs, would request the removal of fire hydrants, and reject calls for better water mains. Perhaps his voice quavered at his conclusion, this self-made, self-reliant man who had striven so hard to make his beloved city safer. "As your chief I was the recipient of your generous confidence and active support; and as long as memory lasts, your kindness will be cherished by me."

On November 3, 1905, Damrell died at his Dover home at the age of seventy-seven. At his funeral on November 6, his Sunday School children strew flowers on his coffin and nearly every superior officer from the Boston Fire Department stood in a line, their heads bared. He was buried in Boston's Forest Hills Cemetery in the city's Jamaica Plain neighborhood, near the Firefighter's Lot, a section of the cemetery reserved for fallen firefighters.

At the grave, Rev. Franklin Hamlin, who had been close to Damrell, said, "He was a self-made man. In his early youth, he was thrown upon his own resources and by a courage that could never be daunted soon gained great success. He was a man of noble presences, courtly manners and graceful speech, yet he was fearless in word."

CHAPTER 15

The Long Slow Sleep of the Fire Fiend

It will be remembered as the great fire, the greatest that America has ever seen, with the exception of that which laid waste Chicago.
—CHARLES "CARLETON" COFFIN
THE STORY OF THE GREAT FIRE, 1872

WITH APOLOGIES TO WRITER CHARLES "CARLETON" COFFIN, THE Great Boston Fire is today a mere flickering in the collective memory of the Hub of the Solar System. "Boston had a fire like Chicago?" is among the common responses to a mention of this fire. How fitting it would be to write that the Great Fire of 1872 immediately changed firefighting forever in Boston and that John S. Damrell took his place among famous Bostonians, was praised to school children, or maybe honored with a statue or two. How wonderful it would be to write that Boston officials used the chance to remake the downtown into large imposing streets that crisscrossed the area in straight, comprehensible patterns with attention to open space and future growth.

It *would* be nice to write that.

Boston's fire safety precautions did increase, but only slowly and with persistent pressure from Damrell and others like him. We can't even say that Boston never had another serious conflagration. What was called the Thanksgiving Day Fire of 1889 broke out during a fierce rainstorm in a six-story granite building at the corner of Bedford and Kingston Streets. A police officer who spotted the fire pulled the alarm in Box 52—yes, the same box used to send the first alarm in the Great Fire—at about 8:00 a.m. Fearing a repeat of the Great Fire, Chief Lewis P.

PORTION OF RUINS OF THE BROWN, DURRELL & CO. BUILDING FROM CORNER OF BEDFORD AND COLUMBIA STREETS, SHOWING RUINS OF AMES BUILDING BEYOND.

Even after the 1872 fire, Boston continued to have conflagrations including a fatal one that broke out on November 28, 1889. Once again Box 52 was pulled to sound the alarm. Photo from "Special Report of the Fire Marshall of the City of Boston on the Kingston-Street Fire, November 28, 1889."

Webber called for help from other departments; sixty-two steam engines responded. The fire raged until the afternoon, burning more than three acres (some of which had been scorched by the Great Fire), destroying a steam fire engine, and causing damages of more than $2 million. Four firemen and a former firefighter were killed.

In light of this new Burnt District, Damrell, then the city's building inspector, called for a meeting of architects, civil engineers, electricians, and builders to discuss building regulations. "Inspector Damrell Says There Are No Fireproof Buildings," read a *Globe* headline on December 4, 1889. Boston was finally ready to seriously consider amending its building codes. National guidelines for buildings, many driven by the national organizations that Damrell pioneered, as well as innovations and improvements in firefighting, diminished the threat of a new Fire Fiend. Bruce Twickler, the documentary filmmaker, came to believe that Damrell was the driving force in making cities around the country safe.

Other changes came slowly to the Boston Fire Department. During the Great Fire, the Amoskeag Manufacturing Company sent one of its newest self-propelled fire engines to Boston, where it apparently performed well. A previous self-propelled engine was purchased in October 1867 and deployed with Engine Company Number Five in East Boston; however, the machine was so noisy it scared horses on the streets and it was sent back in December. After the Great Fire, a representative of Amoskeag wrote to Boston officials to plead for adoption of a self-propelled model, saying these engines really didn't scare horses more than any other engine. Boston apparently did purchase one of the new engines; a self-propelled Amoskeag was stationed at Engine Company 21 in Dorchester until 1877 when it was converted to horse drawn. Firemen were very attached to their horses.

Moreover, in May of 1873, during a test of the capacity of all the city's fire engines, the seven-thousand-pound, second-class self-propelled Amoskeag did not exactly do itself proud. The machine had trouble going uphill and finally ground to a halt in Louisburg Square in the Beacon Hill neighborhood (incidentally, where Louisa May Alcott lived). As firemen attempted to start it, they heard something snap and the engine started rolling down the hill out of control, its velocity increasing with every yard. The men jumped off one by one and the machine came to a stop on Mount Vernon Street. It was undamaged but ran over the foot of fireman James King, breaking several small bones. The other engines had done well and "with the exception of this incident, the entire trial, which was witnessed by the Mayor and a majority of the city government, was entirely successful and satisfactory," the *Boston Globe* reported on May 8. James King might have disagreed.

Others, however, applauded the emergence of self-propelled steam vehicles. A writer in the March 1873 issue of *Our Dumb Animals* was delighted at the idea that "a modified form of steam power will entirely supersede the use of animal power upon our street-railroads." This would help end the abuse of horses, who often suffered from overwork and outright cruelty, the editors argued. The newsletter had already declared that the epizootic had "increased interest in horses and better appreciation of our duty to animals generally." You could argue that cruelty to horses did decrease, but that was because horses would no longer become the country's main form of transportation.

In June of 1897, a new kind of "horseless fire engine" appeared in the city and, according to the *Boston Globe*, horses for the most part "did not seem to mind it in the least." In 1910, the Boston Fire Department purchased its first gasoline-powered motorized vehicles and these gradually replaced the horse-drawn engines. The last fire horses were retired in 1925. The *Boston Sunday Post* ran a heartfelt story on October 14, 1925, about the end of an illustrious career for Buster, Jump, and Dan—"the last of the immortal breed of fire horses to dash through Boston's crowded streets." The reporter mourned that the dramatic sight of horses at full gallop, dragging a steam engine already alight with fire, would never again thrill the young boys of Boston.

What was lost in thrill was gained in faster response time and more and better firefighting innovations. Today's Boston Fire Department—which now covers the Greater Boston area—has fifty-five engine, ladder, tower ladder, and rescue companies. The marine unit has two vessels. There are special operation command units, decontamination units, and technical support units. In 2011, the Boston Fire Department dedicated a new fifty-two-ton fireboat, with five water cannons, capable of shooting about thirteen thousand gallons of water per minute for a distance of 450 feet. It was christened the *John S. Damrell.*

Yet for years, firefighters pondered whether a great fire could happen again. Other communities around Boston have had their own Fire Fends. Chelsea suffered devastating conflagrations in 1908 and 1973, Lynn in 1889, and Salem in 1914. District Chief John Vahey wrote his monograph on the 1872 fire with that possibility in mind. He singled out an incident with Boston Chief of Department John O. Taber, who, as a boy of eight, helped the firemen of Hose Company 2 on Kingston Street in 1872. On the fiftieth anniversary of the fire on November 9, 1922, Taber said, "I believe, as others do, it is correct to say that we are even now with all our apparatus and all our men and all our water supply, not many strides ahead of a conflagration."

Among Boston's firefighting community, the one most schooled in the Great Boston Fire is former Boston Fire Chief and Commissioner Paul Christian. I've known Paul for years, ever since he kindly took pity on a struggling author trying to grasp the intricacies of fire history for her first book. Over the years, Paul has impressed many with his command of fire techniques and the history of the Boston Fire Department; he has long maintained a huge database that includes every company going back to the earliest day.

Not long after Covid-19 shut down person-to-person meetings, I had a Zoom call with Christian to talk about the Great Boston Fire and, in particular, to discuss Damrell's actions. Paul has been interviewed many times about the fire and his nineteenth-century predecessor, and he never fails to speak with passion and insight about the chief engineer, almost as if Damrell were a personal friend and colleague—which, in a way, he is.

Christian sees several key major failures that led to the devastation of the Great Fire. First is the changing nature of the Burnt District from residential to mercantile, with the new four-, five-, and six-story buildings topped by the beautiful but deadly Mansard roofs. These helped create the fire vortex above the streets that was so hard to fight. A second problem was the corroded water mains that were simply too narrow to feed the hoses of the steam fire engines. Christian praises those Victorian-era mechanical workhorses: "They were terrific machines. They could really pump great." However, most of Boston's fire engines were considered second-class engines; the more powerful third-class would have been better. A third factor was that the city had too few hydrants and they were too widely spaced.

A fourth issue was the delay in sending out the alarm. The fire telegraph alarm system, which remains in place today, was an effective system, but the custom of keeping the boxes locked significantly delayed response. The fire may have started even earlier than 7:00 p.m., when people in Charlestown saw a glow in the sky—but the alarm was not struck until 7:24 p.m. This delay was crucial to why the fire could not initially be contained.

The shortage of healthy horses due to the epizootic may have slowed the response time of fire companies, but an examination of the times they arrived revealed the initial companies responding were delayed by two minutes or less. Other companies were delayed by five or ten minutes. What Christian sees as the true fatal flaw was the emergency regulations—put into place on October 26, a few weeks before the fire—that did not call for all six engine companies in Boston proper to respond to Box 52 on the first alarm. If all six engines had responded immediately, that might have made the difference (and rendered this book moot). Even Damrell acknowledged this possibility indirectly in his testimony before the commission investigating the fire when asked whether the first alarm from a bad box (such as Box 52) should have brought in every company. Damrell said, "There are a good many points that, knowing what we know now, we probably should have changed; but from our past experience at that time, knowing the different localities of our city, and the vast number of tinder-boxes which are scattered all over the city, I do not know that I should not, without this present information, do just the same thing again."

It should be noted that Christian vehemently disagrees with the assessment of the commission, which faulted Damrell for staying at the fire scene rather than setting up a command post off the frontlines, perhaps at City Hall. "It's very easy to be critical when it's all over," Christian said. "Damrell didn't have the luxury of portable, two-way radios like we have today, and he had a hard time getting assessments. He was moving around, trying to do the best he could. I would not be critical of that man one bit. I think he did an outstanding job."

As for people who came up to Damrell during the fire to tell him how to do his job, Christian has strong opinions about them as well. If that had happened to him? "I would have them arrested," he said.

Afterword

O vision of that sleepless night,
What hue shall paint the mocking light
That burned and stained the orient skies
Where peaceful morning loves to rise,
As if the sun had lost his way
And dawned to make a second day,
Above how red with fiery glow,
How dark to those it woke below!

"After the Fire"
Oliver Wendell Holmes Sr.

Recently I took a trip to downtown Boston—the first time since the country shut down in March 2020 due to the Covid-19 pandemic. It is still a lively area, even if people are masked and wary of getting too close to each other. I walked the perimeter of the fire, much as photographers John Soule and James Black did in 1872. The crooked streets are a bit wider and straighter than before the Great Fire, although the buildings are much, much taller. Passersby likely thought I was just another tourist with a camera and eyes craning upward, but I was not looking at the buildings that were there, I was trying to imagine what once had been there. The only smoke I smelled was the occasional whiff of marijuana. I wandered over to Box 52 near the intersection where Bedford, Lincoln, and Summer Streets converge. The box is not officially 52 anymore—to the fire department it is Box 1431. It still is labeled 52 on the outside and it is set on a special lamppost. From there, I continued along Summer Street, to Kingston, to the site where the fire began. Once there was a

A special light marks the location of the original Box 52 near the corner of Summer and Kingston Street. The fire alarm box is still labeled 52 but the official number is 1431. PHOTO BY STEPHANIE SCHOROW

historical marker here; there is nothing now. I continued along Summer Street, passing the locations of Hovey's and Trinity Church to Washington Street. I paused by the Old South Meeting House, still a vital historical site, now surrounded by retail outlets. It is the only reminder of the fire that I can find.

As I write this during Covid-19 pandemic, many of us think this country will never be the same, that we have learned lessons about public health and public safety. Yet if someone is reading these words ten, twenty, or even fifty years from now (the vain hope of any history writer) will Covid-19 seem as distant as the Fire Fiend seems today?

Boston has rewritten the story of its downtown many times. The city did not straighten or improve the downtown street grid after the fire, which, Diane Rudnick asserted in her dissertation, blew the chance to revitalize the commercial section. Rudnick, writing from the perspective of the economic doldrums of the 1970s, saw the fire as a failed opportunity to remake Boston. "In these responses to the fire can be seen the signs that a once unique vital creative society had begun the long process of contracting its own horizons," she lamented. But by the 2010s, the downtown area had evolved into one of the city's hottest real estate markets. Today, there are skyscrapers whose heights would make Damrell blanch. Washington Street is lined with theaters, coffee shops, restaurants, and even a grocery store, all of which serve the area's growing number of residents. Jordan Marsh, which took over C.F. Hovey's place in Downtown Crossing in 1947, has itself disappeared, its space taken over by Macy's. Strangely, the downtown is once again becoming a wealthy neighborhood, thanks to the burgeoning luxury condominium market. Burt's magnificent US Post Office Building was finished in 1874 and Post Office Square was created nearby. In 1929, the building was lost—not to fire, but to a wrecking ball, as architectural tastes and space needs changed. The John W. McCormack Post Office and Courthouse now stands on the footprint.

You can walk the streets of downtown Boston all day and find no trace of the Great Fire. Its history lies under the surface, popping up at odd moments. Much of material for this book was found in the archives of the Boston Athenaeum, which was established in 1807 as an independent library to collect books, art, and artifacts. While I was waiting to check into the Athenaeum's elegant building on Beacon Street, a striking painting of a nighttime fire hanging in the foyer caught my eye. I walked closer and was astonished to see this was a rendition of the Great Boston Fire of 1872, painted by F. William Shaw in 1876 and gifted to the Athenaeum in 1986. The perspective is from East Boston. Against a night sky with a faint crescent moon, the fire sends up billowing clouds of peach, rose, and lemon, which light up the city and reflect off the harbor's water. Tiny figures watch transfixed from a dock. It's a glorious, terrible vision. I have seen and collected many images of the fire, but I had never seen this image. And here it is, reminding me of Oliver Wendell Holmes Sr.'s poem on the fire, quoted above.

The Athenaeum staff tell me a story of their own institute's brush with the Fire Fiend. The blaze destroyed the Athenaeum's warehouse on Pearl Street, including a large collection of arms and armor that had been bequeathed in 1869 by Colonel Timothy Bigelow Lawrence. (Perkins made note of this in his detailed descriptions of the losses to art and culture in the fire). The armor was intended to grace the halls of the new Museum of Fine Arts in Boston, founded in 1870. Fortunately, about twenty-eight items from the Lawrence collection were stored elsewhere and did ultimately go to the museum. When Mrs. Lawrence heard of the fire, she reportedly said, "There is no armor against fate," and I fervently hope she actually said this. The Athenaeum has one memento of this loss, the key to the storeroom in the Pearl Street warehouse.

While downtown Boston forgets, firefighters and fire buffs do not. The Box 52 Association, one of the nation's oldest fire buff organizations, was founded in 1912 and incorporated in 1918. It was, the *Boston Globe* wrote on December 13, 1912, "composed entirely of men who taken an extraordinary interest in firemen and fires [and includes] very prominent men who would rather miss a meal than miss being present at a large fire, no matter at what hours it might occur or how severe the weather should be." Today, the association continues to meet regularly to discuss fire issues and promote fire protection. The Boston Sparks Association, another fire buff group, runs the Boston Fire Museum in South Boston, which also keeps alive the story of the Great Fire. The story goes that rubble from the fire was used as landfill and the Boston Fire Museum sits on this landfill. The Boston Fire Historical Society (of which I was a founding member) maintains a web site (bostonfirehistory.org), where you may read the Boston Fire Department annual reports of 1871, 1872, and 1873 and ponder Damrell's own words. Indeed, the "spark," or fire buff, has a long history in Boston; the beloved conductor of the Boston Pops Orchestra, Arthur Fielder, was an avid spark who would travel in his own vehicle to large fires at any time of the day or night to watch Boston firefighters at work. He was even made an "Honorary Captain" in the Boston Fire Department. He was also a collector of antique fire-fighting helmets and material; much of his collection was donated to the Boston Fire Museum.

The Bare Cove Fire Museum in Hingham, Massachusetts, has artifacts believed to be collected from the ruins of the fire. At the time, enterprising youths attempted to sell souvenirs gleaned from the wreckage. PHOTO BY STEPHANIE SCHOROW

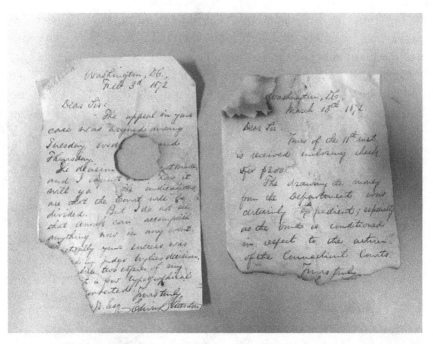

Two burned letters, believed to be from the ruins of the Great Fire in the collection of the Bare Cove Fire Museum in Hingham, Massachusetts. PHOTO BY STEPHANIE SCHOROW

Some years ago, when I gave a talk on fires at the Bare Cove Fire Museum in Hingham, Massachusetts, the staff pulled out a box containing, according to the handwriting on a fading orange card, "artifacts collected by Hingham historian George Lincoln after the 1872 disaster." It held dusty pieces of melted and fused glass, fragments of two letters, burned like toast around the edges, dated February 3, 1872, and March 13, 1872, and a formal photographic portrait in a scorched frame. In the photo, a woman's face framed by bobbed hair peers out from behind cracked glass; her eyes look away from the camera, as if, perhaps, the fire in the far distance catches her attention. There were many references in the research about "souvenirs" sold by enterprising boys after the fire, perhaps they were tossed out over the years or sit in dusty boxes. Some apparently survived. I held some of the bits and pieces from the museum and tried to imagine the inferno that nearly consumed them.

In 2012, a partially restored Kearsarge turned to Boston for a day, sponsored by the Boston Fire History Society, which tried to place the machine in the general location where its company fought the fire 140 years before. PHOTO BY STEPHANIE SCHOROW

After the fire, the Kearsarge Company 3 returned to a hero's welcome in Portsmouth. Overhauled in 1888, the engine continued to operate until early in the twentieth century. In 1925 it was sold for $60. For decades it languished in a shed, slowly rusting. It was eventually purchased by a collector, refurbished by notable fire apparatus restorer Andy Swift of Hope, Maine, and was repurchased by the Portsmouth Fire Department for display. Through the efforts of the Boston Fire Historical Society, the Kearsarge returned to Boston in November 2012 as part of a Fire History Month event. For a day, the machine sat outside the Old South Meeting House, the site of its great triumph, in all its steampunk splendor. Only a few passersby realized the significance of that example of Victorian technology. It is now back with the Portsmouth Fire Department.

We continually re-evaluate the past in terms of the present as diaries or artifacts are uncovered, as science reorients our knowledge of anatomy or disease, or as we speculate on continued consequences of decisions made decades or even centuries ago. Louisa May Alcott's work is experiencing a popular revival, while Oliver Wendell Holmes Sr.'s image has been tarnished by a historically embarrassing fact. While he was dean of Harvard Medical School in 1850, the school revoked the acceptance of the school's three Black students, citing concerns of interracial mixing. Holmes was not alone in reflecting the racial bias of the day—it was likely not solely his decision to exclude the students—but that moral failure casts a pall over the legacy of an otherwise distinguished career. By contrast, abolitionist William Lloyd Garrison's uncompromising stance on slavery remains truly visionary.

Thanks to improvements in building codes, construction techniques, fire sprinklers, home smoke detectors, and better response communication, Boston does not suffer from fires to the same extent it once did, although tragic deaths and property damage continue to haunt us. The Great Fire, thus, presents another kind of lesson; we may not worry about fires as much as we did—at least not in cities, the danger has shifted to forests and rural areas. Yet Damrell's warnings of what *could* happen should we face a worst-case scenario are as timely now as ever.

Even though I am writing about events that happened 150 years ago, I can't help but see them through the lens of daily life in 2020 and 2021. What lessons will we draw from the past two years facing Covid-19? And which will we forget?

NOTES

PROLOGUE

The direct quotes were taken from word-for-word testimony by John S. Damrell in the *Report of the Commissioners Appointed to Investigate the Cause and Management of the Great Fire in Boston* (Boston: Rockwell & Churchill, 1873; https://archive.org/details/reportofcommissi1873bost/page/614/mode/2up).

INTRODUCTION

Details on nineteenth-century fires from Margaret Hindle Hazen and Robert M. Hazen, *Keepers of the Flame: The Role of Fire in American Culture: 1775-1925* (Princeton: Princeton University Press, 1992).

CHAPTER 1

Description of Boston in the 1870s from Stephen Puleo's *A City So Grand: The Rise of an American Metropolis, Boston 1850-1900* (Boston: Beacon Press, 2011). The historian with a flair for overstatement was Charles "Carleton" Coffin, author of *The Story of the Great Fire* (Boston: Shepard and Gill, 1872). Information on the organization of the Boston Fire Department came from Diane Tarmy Rudnick, *Boston and the Fire of 1872: The Stillborn Phoenix* (Boston University, 1971); James Kellar Bugbee, "Fires and Fire Departments," *North American Review*, 1873; John Vahey, *The Epizootic Fire*, monograph, 1972; and Boston Fire Historical Society (bostonfirehistory.org). Comments by Charles Bird and A.C. Martin from *Report of the Commissioners Appointed to Investigate the Cause and Management of the Great Fire in Boston*. Details on the 1870 Jubilee from "Big Boom in Boston," by Rufus Jarman, *American Heritage*, October 1969. Steam engine history from "How Steam Blew the Rowdies Out of The Fire Departments" by Robert S. Holzman, *American Heritage*, December 1955. Fire alarm telegraph details from Stephanie Schorow's

Boston on Fire: A History of Fires and Firefighting in Boston (Beverly: Commonwealth Editions, 2003).

CHAPTER 2

Details on Damrell's family history was drawn from unpublished material in the Bruce Twickler archive; information posted at www.boston1872 .docema.com/Damrell_timeline.html; and Damrell's entry in *Men of Progress: One Thousand Biographical Sketches and Portraits of Leaders in Business and Professional Life in the Commonwealth of Massachusetts* (Boston: *New England Magazine*, 1896). Other details on Damrell's life from obituaries in *Boston Transcript*, November 4, 1905, and *Boston Globe*, November 4, 7, and 8, 1905. Damrell's election as chief is based on an account in Arthur Wellington Brayley, *A Complete History of the Boston Fire Department* (Boston: J. P. Daley, 1889). Details of Boston's government from John W. Decrow, "The Great Boston Fire" (Bureau of Commercial and Industrial Affairs, Boston Chamber of Commerce, 1922). Information on expenditures and organization of the Boston Fire Department were taken from Rudnick's *Boston and the Fire of 1872: The Stillborn Phoenix*. Other information on the Boston Fire Department from Vahey, *The Epizootic Fire;* Bugbee, "Fires and Fire Departments," *North American Review; Report of the Commissioners Appointed to Investigate the Cause and Management of the Great Fire in Boston*; and the 1870, 1871, 1872 annual Boston Fire Department reports posted at bostonfirehistory.org.

CHAPTER 3

Details on the Chicago fire from Charles F. Haywood, *General Alarm: A Dramatic Account of Fires and Firefighting in America* (New York: Dodd, Mead & Company, 1967). Garrison letters were quoted from *The Letters of William Lloyd Garrison: To Rouse the Slumbering Land 1868-1879* (Cambridge: Belknap Press of Harvard University Press, 1981). Damrell's account of his 1871 trip to Chicago was drawn from "Report of Chief Engineer Damrell to the Officers of the Boston Fire Department in Relation to Trip to Chicago, After its Destruction by Fire, October 7th, 8th, and 9th 1871," reproduced in *Box 52 Newsletter*, No. 48. The history of the Boston's water system was found at "Water system history" posted

on the Massachusetts Water Resources Authority website (www.mwra
.com/04water/html/hist1.htm); and Rudnick's *Boston and the Fire of
1872: The Stillborn Phoenix.* Background on building codes from Rudnick,
Brayley, *A Complete History of the Boston Fire Department,* and Charles
Damrell, *A Half Century of Boston's Buildings* (Boston: L.P. Hager, 1895).
"Chicago was garish, insubstantial, inflammable" quote is from Rudnick.
Thorndike's denials are from Rudnick. Details of Damrell's fights with
the water board are from Robert Taylor, "The Great Boston Fire, 1872: A
Disaster with a Villain: Old-Style Politics," *Boston Sunday Globe,* Novem-
ber 12, 1972; and testimony in *Report of the Commissioners Appointed to
Investigate the Cause and Management of the Great Fire in Boston.*

CHAPTER 4
Sources for this chapter include an interview with Sean Kheraj, Septem-
ber 30, 2020; Kheraj's "The Great Epizootic of 1872–73: Networks of
Animal Disease in North American Urban Environments," *Environ-
mental History,* April 25, 2018; and Sister Denise Granger's "The Horse
Distemper of 1872 and its Effect on Urban Transportation," *Historical
Journal of Massachusetts,* Volume 2, No. 1, Spring 1973. Details on the
October 26, 1872, meeting from John Vahey's *The Epizootic Fire.* Descrip-
tions of sick horses from Sylvester Baxter, "A Reporter's Memory of
Boston's Great Fire," *Boston Herald,* October 21, 1922; John Damrell's
"Address to the Boston Veteran Firemen," February 2, 1886; *Our Dumb
Animals,* newsletter, November 1872 and December 1872; talk by Anne
Green on December 1, 2011, "How Horses Shaped American History
and Why It Matters That They Did" at the Philadelphia Society for Pro-
moting Agriculture (pspaonline.com/resources/meetings/12-01-11); and
Alfred Downes's, *Firefighters and their Pets* (New York: Harper Broth-
ers, 1907). Medical details from Adoniram B. Judson's "History and the
Course of the Epizootic Among Horses on the North American Conti-
nent in 1872-1873," Public Health Reports and Papers, presented at the
Meeting of the American Public Health Association, 1873; and James
Law, "Equine Influenza Epidemic of 1872" *Report of the U.S. Commis-
sioner of Agriculture for the Year 1872* (en.wikisource.org/wiki/Equine_
Influenza_Epidemic_of_1872). Other details from *Harper's Weekly,* "The

Horse Epidemic," November 16, 1872. Excerpts from *Our Dumb Animals* newsletters accessed via https://books.google.com/books/about/Our_Dumb_Animals.html?id=EEcsAAAAYAAJ.

CHAPTER 5

Descriptions of press dinner from Sylvester Baxter's "A Reporter's Memory of Boston's Great Fire," *Boston Herald,* October 21, 1922, and Robert G. Fitch, "The Great Boston Fire of 1872," *New England Magazine,* Volume 2, September 1989–February 1900. Fire descriptions are from Conwell's, *History of the Great Fire in Boston, November 9 and 10, 1872;* Coffin's *The Story of the Great Fire;* and F.E. Frothingham, *The Boston Fire, November 8th and 10th, 1872* (Boston: Lee & Shepard Publishers, 1873). Eyewitness accounts of the fire, including Damrell's, were drawn from *Report of the Commissioners Appointed to Investigate the Cause and Management of the Great Fire in Boston.* Other details are from Lucius Beebe, *Boston and the Boston Legend* (New York: D-Appleton Century, 1935).

CHAPTER 6

Sources for this chapter include Margaret D. Williams, "My Grandpa and the Boston Fire of 1872," Manchester, New Hampshire, *Union Leader,* June 14, 1992; details on firefighting from *Report of the Commissioners Appointed to Investigate the Cause and Management of the Great Fire in Boston;* (Conwell, *History of the Great Fire in Boston, November 9 and 10, 1872;* Frothingham, *The Boston Fire, November 8th and 10th, 1872*); Decrow, "The Great Boston Fire" (Bureau of Commercial and Industrial Affairs, Boston Chamber of Commerce, 1922); *Boston Transcript,* November 11, 1872; and Baxter's "A Reporter's Memory of Boston's Great Fire," *Boston Herald.* I also relied on the map of the fire's progress created by Bruce Twickler, which shows the spread of the fire, lists the arrival of the fire companies, and contains other details of the Great Fire. Information from this map was used in a chapter on the fire in *The Atlas of Boston History,* edited by Nancy Seasholes (University of Chicago Press: 2019).

Chapter 7

Sources for this chapter include articles in the *Boston Globe*, November 11 and 12, 1872; Brayley, *A Complete History of the Boston Fire Department*; Conwell, History of the Great Fire in Boston, November 9 and 10, 1872; Lucius Beebe, *Boston and the Boston Legend* (New York: D-Appleton Century, 1935). Benjamin P. Pickering's testimony from page 164 of the *Report of the Commissioners Appointed to Investigate the Cause and Management of the Great Fire in Boston.* Clara's story appeared in several accounts, including in *Harper's Weekly*, November 20, 1872; details on Charles Eliot and Paul Adams from Rudnick's *Boston and the Fire of 1872: The Stillborn Phoenix*; details on Patrick Donahoe from "The Richest and Most Influential Catholic in New England: The Pilot's Patrick Donahoe Lived a Rags-to-Riches Saga—Twice," by Peter Stevens, *Boston Irish Reporter*, October 31, 2001. Other descriptions of the fire came from the unnamed authors of History of the Great Conflagration or Boston and Its Destruction (Philadelphia: William Flint & Co., 1872). Sections of Garrison letters were from *The Letters of William Lloyd Garrison: To Rouse the Slumbering Land 1868-1879.* Alcott letters are from *The Selected Letters of Louisa May Alcott* (Boston: Little, Brown and Company 1987). Quotes from Phillip Brooks from Alexander V. G. Allen's *Life and Letters of Phillip Brooks* (New York: E.P. Dutton and Company, 1900); quotes from Oliver Wendell Holmes Sr. from John T. Morse's *Life and Letters of Oliver Wendell Holmes* (Boston: Houghton, Mifflin and Company, 1896). The sad story of Alexander Graham Bell's lost description of the fire is from his letters of November. 11, 12, 19, 1872, in Alexander Graham Bell Family Papers at the Library of Congress (loc.gov/collections/alexander-graham-bell-papers/about-this-collection) and "Bell Writes of Devastating Boston Fire," Brantford Expositor, October 14, 2017.

Chapter 8

Details on the number of companies at the fire from Decrow, "The Great Boston Fire"; James Gowan's story was cited in a 1975 letter from Biddeford Fire Department from author's files. Details, conversations, and description of the use of gunpowder are from testimony from Damrell, Burt, and Woolley in the *Report of the Commissioners Appointed to*

Investigate the Cause and Management of the Great Fire in Boston, and Robert Taylor, "The Great Boston Fire, 1872: A Disaster with a Villain: Old-Style Politics," *Boston Sunday Globe,* November 12, 1972. Higginson's recollections from *Report of the Commissioners Appointed to Investigate the Cause and Management of the Great Fire in Boston* and Alissa Perry, "Life and Letters of Henry Lee Higginson," *Atlantic Monthly Press,* 1921. Grace Revere's account is from "Letter of Eyewitness," *Boston Transcript,* November 7, 1936. Other fire details are from Harold Murdock, *Gentleman in Boston: Letters written by a Gentleman in Boston to his Friends in Paris: describing the Great Fire* (Boston: Houghton Mifflin Company, 1909) and "The Great Boston Fire and Some Contributing Causes," a paper read to the Bostonian Society on November 19, 1912. Burt's account of the fire is taken from his journal archived by the Bostonian Society, posted on boston1872.docema.com/letters_GeneralBurt.html, and his bio in Twickler archives. Fire descriptions are from Conwell, *History of the Great Fire in Boston, November 9 and 10, 1872.* Details on Hovey's are from "Shopping Days in Retro Boston," shoppingdaysinretroboston.blogspot.com/2011/05/looking-back-at-cf-hoveys-of-boston.html. C.F. Hovey Company Business Records, 1837–1920 (Harvard Business School; web.archive.org/web/20100622002001/http:/www.library.hbs.edu/hc/sfa/cfhovey.htm); "The History of the house of Hovey [microform]: containing some interesting reminiscences of almost three quarters of a century," (archive.org/stream/historyofhouseof00cfho/historyofhouseof00cfho_djvu.txt).

CHAPTER 9

Information on the Kearsarge from Harold Murdock, *Gentleman in Boston* and "The Great Boston Fire," in the minutes of the Bostonian Society's Proceedings. Thomas Marvin's account is from in the *Portsmouth Daily Chronicle,* February 1, 1916, and William S. Hazen's account in the March 7, 1916, *Portsmouth Daily Chronicle.* Letters to the Editor in the *Chronicle* indicated some Portsmouth firemen disputed that the Kearsarge company should get credit for saving the Old South. Other Kearsarge history from City of Portsmouth, files.cityofportsmouth.com/

fires/history.pdf, and Baxter's "A Reporter's Memory of Boston's Great Fire," *Boston Herald.*

CHAPTER 10

This chapter relied heavily on the meticulous research of Michael J. Novak's *Photography and the Great Fire of November 1872,* monograph, 3rd revised edition, 1992. Also Stephen Robert Edidin, *The Photographs of James Wallace Black* (Williams College Museum of Art, 1977). Quotes from Black from "The Boston Fire," *Philadelphia Photographer,* December 1872. Information on stenography and Oliver Wendell Holmes Sr.'s role in its development from "Stereographs were the Original Virtual Reality," by Clive Thomas, *Smithsonian Magazine,* October 2017, and Holmes's article, "The Stereoscope and the Stereograph," *Atlantic Monthly,* June 1859. Additional details on illustrators from: Nineteenth-Century Newspaper Analytics (ncna.dh.chass.ncsu.edu/imageanalytics/history.php); American Antiquarian Society's "The News Media and the Making of America, 1730-1865, (americanantiquarian.org/earlyamericannewsmedia); the Magazinist, (themagazinist.com/uploads/Harpers_Weekly.pdf); Norman Rockwell Museum, Illustration History Late 19th Century (www.illustrationhistory.org/history/time-periods/late-19th-century); and "On This Day," *New York Times* (archive.nytimes.com/www.nytimes.com/learning/general/onthisday/harp/1130.html).

CHAPTER 11

Stories on opening safes from Conwell, *History of the Great Fire in Boston*, Beebe, *Boston and the Boston Legend*, and W. F. Chandler and Co., *Chandler & Co.'s full account of the great fire in Boston and the ruins* (Boston: W.H. Chandler & Co., 1872). Details on losses of medieval torture devices and antique armor from Augustus Thorndike Perkins, *Losses to Literature and the Fine Arts by The Great Fire in Boston: Prepared for the New England Historic Genealogical Society* (Boston: Press of David Clapp & Son, 1873). Details on firemen's deaths from Boston Fire Department Annual Report, 1872; Brayley, *A Complete History of the Boston Fire Department;* and articles from the *Boston Globe,* November 21 and 28, 1872. Insurance information from Rudnick's *Boston and the Fire of 1872:*

The Stillborn Phoenix; Frothingham's *The Boston Fire*, November 8th and 10th, 1872; and *Report of the Commissioners Appointed to Investigate the Cause and Management of the Great Fire in Boston*. Details on Boston's paradoxical attitude on relief was explored in depth by Rudnick. Damrell's letter to the family or widow of a firefighter is from the collection of Paul Christian.

CHAPTER 12

Word-for-word testimony is from *Report of the Commissioners Appointed to Investigate the Cause and Management of the Great Fire in Boston*. Other details from Taylor, "The Great Boston Fire, 1872: A Disaster with a Villain: Old-Style Politics."

CHAPTER 13

Many of the details on Boston's rebuilding and subsequent political battles are from Christine Meisner, *The Limits of Power: Great Fires and the Process of City Growth in America* (Cambridge: Cambridge University Press, 1986); Rudnick, *Boston and the Fire of 1872: The Stillborn Phoenix*; and Frothingham's *The Boston Fire, November 8th and 10th, 1872*. Details on Patrick Donahoe from "The Richest and Most Influential Catholic in New England: The Pilot's Patrick Donahoe Lived a Rags-to-Riches Saga — Twice," by Peter Stevens, *Boston Irish Reporter*, October 31, 2001, and Robert G. Fitch's "The Great Boston Fire of 1872," *New England Magazine*, Volume 2, September 1989–February 1900. Bradlee's success in rebuilding Boston was found at www.danversstatehospital.org/nathaniel -bradlee and www.bahistory.org/HistoryNathanielBradlee.html. Information about Sylvester Baxter's later life from The Cultural Landscape Foundation tclf.org/pioneer/sylvester-baxter, Karl Haglund's "Emerald Metropolis," *Arnoldia;* "Boston's Metropolitan Past: Baxter & Eliot's 1893 Plan," *Urban Nature* (Cambridge: Massachusetts Institute of Technology); and Haglund's chapter in *The Atlas of Boston History*, edited by Nancy Seasholes, University of Chicago Press: 2019.

CHAPTER 14

Sources for this chapter include my interview with Bruce Twickler in November 2020 and www.boston1872.docema.com/Damrell_timeline .html; Damrell's "Address to the Boston Veteran Firemen," February 2, 1886; and obituaries in *Boston Transcript*, November 4, 1905, and *Boston Globe*, November 4, 7, and 8, 1905. Vineyard Haven fire details are from www.history.vineyard.net.

CHAPTER 15

This chapter was based on interview with former Boston Fire Commissioner Paul Christian, April 23, 2020; Vahey, *The Epizootic Fire*, monograph, 1972; and Decrow, "The Great Boston Fire." Details on the 1889 Thanksgiving Day fire from "Special Report of the Fire Marshall of the City of Boston on the Kingston Street Fire, November 28, 1889" (Boston: Rockwell and Churchill). Information on the modern Boston Fire Department from its web site at.boston.gov/departments/fire-operations/how-fire-department-works

AFTERWORD

Information on the Boston Athenaeum's key to its burned warehouse from *Acquired Tastes: 200 Years of Collecting for the Boston Athenaeum* (Boston: University Press of New England, 2006)

Further Reading

A note on sources: Much of the verbatim dialogue was take from *Report of the Commissioners Appointed to Investigate the Cause and Management of the Great Fire in Boston* (Boston: Rockwell & Churchill, 1873; https:// archive.org/details/reportofcommissi1873bost/page/614/mode/2up).

Many thanks go to Bruce Twickler, who shared his files on the fire and whose map of the fire's progression was invaluable in tracking the fire spread and detailing the arrival times of the fire companies. Much of Twickler's immense work on the fire can be found at https://www.boston 1872.docema.com, including additional maps, memoirs, letters, photos, and Boston directories.

The website of the Boston Fire Historical Society (firehistory.org) is an incredible repository of material related to the Boston Fire Department and Boston fire history.

Other online sources include the Boston Public Library, from which photos showing in vivid detail the extent of the fire were obtained.

Through the Library of Congress Research Guide (https://guides.loc .gov/chronicling-america-great-boston-fire), I was able to access newspapers from around the country for their coverage of the Boston Fire.

I relied heavily on the archives of the *Boston Globe*, *Harper's Weekly*, issues of November 16, 23, 30, and December 7, 1872; *The London Illustrated News*, issue of Nov. 30, 1872; and articles from the *Boston Herald*, the *Boston Transcript*, the *Boston Advertiser*, and the *Boston Post*.

Annual Reports of the Boston Fire Department, 1867, 1868, 1869, 1870, 1871, and 1872, accessed at bostonfirehistory.org

Alcott, Louisa May, *The Selected Letters of Louisa May Alcott* (Boston: Little, Brown and Company 1987).

Beebe, Lucius, *Boston and the Boston Legend* (New York: D-Appleton Century, 1935)

Brayley, Arthur Wellington, *A Complete History of the Boston Fire Department: including the fire-alarm service and the protective department from 1630 to 1888* (Boston: J. P. Daley, 1889).

Baxter, Sylvester, "A Reporter's Memory of Boston's Great Fire," *The Boston Herald*, October 21, 1922.

Bugbee, James Kellar, "Fires and Fire Departments," *North American Review*, 1873.

W. F. Chandler and Co., Chandler & Co.'s full account of the great fire in Boston and the ruins (Boston: W.H. Chandler & Co., 1872).

Christian, Paul and the Boston Fire Historical Society, *Boston's Fire Trail: A Walk Through the City's Fire and Firefighting History* (Charleston, S.C.: The History Press, 2007).

Coffin, Charles "Carleton," *The Story of the Great Fire* (Boston: Shepard, and Gill, 1872).

Conwell, Russell Herman, *History of the Great Fire in Boston, November 9 and 10, 1872* (Boston: B.B. Russell Philadelphia, Quaker-City Publishing House, 1873).

Damrell, Charles Stanhope, *A Half Century of Boston's Buildings* (Boston: L.P. Hager, 1895).

Decrow, John W., "The Great Boston Fire," Bureau of Commercial and Industrial Affairs, Boston Chamber of Commerce, 1922.

Downes, Alfred, *Firefighters and Their Pets* (New York: Harper & Brothers, 1907).

Edidin, Stephen Robert, *The Photographs of James Wallace Black* (Williams College Museum of Art, 1977).

Fitch, Robert G., "The Great Boston Fire of 1872," *New England Magazine*, Volume 2, September 1989-February 1900.

Frothingham, F. E., *The Boston Fire, November 8th and 10th, 1872* (Boston: Lee & Shepard Publishers, 1873).

Granger, Sister Denise, "The Horse Distemper of 1872 and its Effect on Urban Transportation," *Historical Journal of Massachusetts*, Volume 2, No 1 (Spring 1973).

Kheraj, Sean, "The Great Epizootic of 1872-1873: Networks of Animal Disease in North American Urban Environments," *Environmental History*, April 25, 2018, 495–521.

Haywood, Charles F., General Alarm: A Dramatic Account of Fires and Fire-Fighting in America (New York: Dodd, Mead & Company, 1967).

Hazen, Margaret Hindle and Robert M. Hazen, *Keepers of the Flame: The Role of Fire in American Culture: 1775-1925* (Princeton: Princeton University Press, 1992).

History of the Great Conflagration or Boston and Its Destruction (Philadelphia: William Flint & Co., 1872).

Hornbeck, Richard and Daniel Keniston, "Creative Destruction: Barriers to Urban Growth and the Great Boston Fire of 1872," *American Economic Review*, 2017.

Merrill, Walter M. and Louis Ruchames, editors, *The Letters of William Lloyd Garrison: To Rouse the Slumbering Land 1868-1879* (Cambridge: Belknap Press of Harvard University Press, 1981).

Morse Jr, John T., "Account of the Great Boston Fire in a letter to John Lothrop Motley," in *Oliver Wendell Holmes, Life and Letters* (Boston: Houghton Mifflin, 1896).

Murdock, Harold, *Gentleman in Boston: Letters Written by a Gentleman in Boston to his Friends in Paris: Describing the Great Fire* (Boston: Houghton Mifflin Co., 1909).

———"The Great Boston Fire," a paper read to the Bostonian Society on November 19, 1912, and contained in the January 2, 1913, minutes of the society.

Novak, Michael J., *Photography and the Great Fire of November 1872*, monograph, 3rd revised edition, 1992.

Perkins, Augustus Thorndike, *Losses to Literature and the Fine Arts by The Great Fire in Boston: Prepared for the New England Historic Genealogical Society* (Boston: Press of David Clapp & Son, 1873).

Puleo, Stephen, *A City So Grand: The Rise of an American Metropolis, Boston 1850-1900* (Boston: Beacon Press, 2011).

Rosen, Christine Meisner, *The Limits of Power: Great Fires and the Process of City Growth in America* (Cambridge: Cambridge University Press, 1986).

Report of the Commissioners Appointed to Investigate the Cause and Management of the Great Fire in Boston (Boston: Rockwell & Churchill, 1873).

Rudnick, Diane Tarmy, *Boston and the Fire of 1872: The Stillborn Phoenix* (Boston University, 1971).

Schorow, Stephanie, *Boston on Fire: A History of Fires and Firefighting in Boston* (Beverly: Commonwealth Editions, 2003).

Taylor, Robert, "The Great Boston Fire, 1872: A Disaster with a Villain: Old-Style Politics," Boston: *Boston Sunday Globe,* November 1972.

Twickler, Bruce, producer and writer, *Damrell's Fire,* documentary, 2006; materials posted at http://boston1872.docema.com, including "Timeline of John Stanhope Damrell," "Memories of Boston's Great Fire of 1872," which has an account of the fire written by William L. Burt; and "Boston 1872: Maps and Streets." Also: "Teachers' Guide for Damrell's Fire," and "Damrell's Learning Resources," and biographical material on John Damrell from unpublished manuscript.

Vahey, John, *The Epizootic Fire,* monograph, 1972.

Index

Acknowledgments

A book like this cannot be completed without the help of libraries, histori-cal societies and groups devoted to keeping history alive and relevant. I am extremely grateful to the members of the Boston Fire Historical Society, particularly society president Ted Gerber, who provided me with much needed material. I am also grateful to former firefighters Paul Christian and Bill Noonan for reading this manuscript and who always have been so generous to a fire-fighting neophyte like me. Bruce Twickler deserves great praise for extraordinary work on his documentary on the fire and for his foresight and generosity in making so many materials available on the Docema website – also for his excellent comments on a draft of this manuscript. Many thanks to the staff of the Boston Athenaeum and the Boston Public Library. I am grateful to Sean Kheraj for generously agreeing to speak to me about his research on the epizootic. I also had assistance from Brian Wood, curator of the Bell Homestead National Historic Site, Tom Leland of the *Boston Globe,* and Aaron Schmidt of the Boston Public Library. I must thank my two writing groups—the Med-ford Writers group and Works in Progress—for their encouragement and extremely helpful critiques. Above all else, I have to thank my extraordi-nary first editor Anne Stuart, who somehow cleaned up a messy manu-script with incredible efficiency and creativity. I will always be grateful for the support of my family and friends (and cats) for helping me keep my spirits up during the long slog to the finish. Many thanks to Amy Lyons and the copy editors of Globe Pequot for shepherding me through the publication process.

About the Author

Stephanie Schorow has written eight nonfiction books on Boston history, including *Inside the Combat Zone: The Stripped-Down Story of Boston's Most Notorious Neighborhood, Drinking Boston: A History of the City and its Spirits, The Cocoanut Grove Fire, Boston on Fire: A History of Fires and Firefighting in Boston, East of Boston: Notes from the Harbor Island*, and *The Crime of the Century: How the Brink's Robbers Stole Millions and the Hearts of Boston*. With co-author Beverly Ford, she wrote *The Boston Mob Guide: Hit Men, Hoodlums and Hangouts*. She also served as the editor of *Boston's Fire Trail* with the Boston Fire Historical Society. She has worked as an editor and reporter for the *Boston Herald* and other newspapers, as well as the Associated Press.